# You are not
# BOSSY,
## you are your own
# BOSS

Management and leadership strategies

Catherine Tuitt MBE LLB HONS

**BALBOA**.PRESS
A DIVISION OF HAY HOUSE

Balboa Press books may be ordered through booksellers or by contacting:

Balboa Press
A Division of Hay House
1663 Liberty Drive
Bloomington, IN 47403
www.balboapress.co.uk
UK TFN: 0800 0148647 (Toll Free inside the UK)
UK Local: (02) 0369 56325 (+44 20 3695 6325 from outside the UK)

Print information available on the last page.

ISBN: 978-1-9822-8683-5 (sc)
ISBN: 978-1-9822-8682-8 (e)

Balboa Press rev. date: 02/08/2023

# CONTENTS

# BIOGRAPHY OF AUTHOR

**C** **ATHERINE TUITT MBE LLB Hons** is the author of You are not bossy; you are your own boss - Management and leadership strategies.

Catherine is a legal adviser, business consultant, and motivational speaker.

Catherine studied management and leadership and earned a university law degree and a higher diploma in Forensic Science.

Catherine studied in London and Jerusalem in the Middle east. She was a chief executive officer and director of a multi-million pound charity.

Catherine also, for her hobby, creates and designs unique clothing and is a keen photographer and filmmaker. She uses her art and nutrition as a resource to assist clients overcoming trauma and rebuilding their lives.

Catherine was awarded a national honour in 2021 by Her Majesty Queen Elizabeth for her contribution to charities and community service that has had a lasting positive impact on United Kingdom citizens lives.

# DEDICATION

This book is dedicated to my late mother, Lena Tuitt. She sacrificed so much for me to excel. To Marcus Tuitt, Helena Tuitt and Joshua Wright, and Octavia Wright. I think of you always, and you have inspired me in your absence or presence. Love you all x.

# BIBLIOGRAPHY

Miler. R, Parrow, J, Walker D 1992 A calculus of mobile processes I & II information & computation. Book

Wikipedia source - Sir Alan Sugar, Roman Abramovich, Rupert Murdoch.

Mintzberg model Henry Mintzberg.

Locke Edwin. Goal setting theory.

KPIs Professor Peter Drucker.

Zade, L.A 1965 Fuzzy sets, information and control 12. Book

Nonaka, I. Takeuchi, H 1995 The knowledge creating company. Book

Kappe. F 2001 Knowledge management with the hyperwave. Article

Tutill, G.S 1990 eKnowledge infrastructure. Book

Cognitive solutions 2004 Data hierarchy model Internet source/article

Business balls 2012 Computer information system models. Article Internet webpage

Business balls 2012 Thought leadership, management Gurus. Article

Business balls 2012 Personality theories and types. Article Mind tools 2012 Giving feedback. Article

Dulewicz, professor Victor PHD Dulewicz. V.A. (1995) article validation of Belbin's team roles using bosses rating of competence. Book Journal of occupational and organisational psychology. Journal.

A review of Leadership theory and competency frameworks centre for leadership studies. Review online.

National college for school leadership 1999.

Higgs report on non - executive directors.

Chartered institute for personnel development, London 1997

101 ways to improve your business - John Fenton 1990 Robert

Black and Jane Mortoon 1963.

Belbin R. Management teams: Why they succeed or fail.

2010 Isa Luminous project graphic designer.

# CHAPTER 1

# CURRENT ISSUES IMPACTING
# ON THE ROLE OF LEADERS

C urrent technological advancements over the latter part of the century led to the role of leaders being trained in the latest Information technology and software being at the forefront of the skills base required for leadership roles.

Particularly not many organisations prefer those they appoint to be proficient in computer technology and self – administering.

More and more leaders choose to allow their teams to work from home and virtual offices in remote parts of the globalisation of the workforce, where some projects may be located in other areas.

This means that the regulation of these parts of the business present other challenges for control and regulation as they may cover different jurisdictions and have different laws and bodies that enforce breaches.

Compliance means conforming to a rule, such as a specification, policy, or standards which can vary in different countries and states.

There are also levels of criminal responsibility, which carry different penalties, and these have to be monitored, particularly if managing a financial sector regulated workplace.

Areas such as Anti money laundering, political corruption, Terrorist financing, Anti- corruption, Foreign corrupt practices act, and due diligence.

Also, in the security industry or a law firm leader, the partners must regulate the staff to ensure they comply with the laws. The organisation can be fined due to criminal compliance failure if breached.

Partnerships & Alliances

The value chain of involvement with others provides leaders working with alliances and partnerships with the advantage of combining resources and sharing a customer base, without the potential disadvantages of control dilution and cultural resistance.

Strategic alliances can establish formidable business groupings that are flexible and responsive and where the interests of the individual partnerships are reflected in the interests of the alliances as a whole.

Mergers and takeovers

One company may wish to take over or merge with another to enhance its operation or eliminate competition. This means leaders have a larger pool of skills coming into the team without having to recruit and also train the existing staff,

Acquire an on-going business rather than start from scratch. The disadvantage of being a leader could be the fact that you now have to deal with a group of individuals who may have mixed feelings about the takeover or merger and not be fully committed to the organisation.

Leadership

The Positive aspects of balancing many roles and carrying them out via communication technologies. This is also not limited to location, which enables the leadership of a large geographic area if required. It is no different from any other form of effective leadership.

It requires a high level of transformational leadership because of the highly participative nature of the e - world between e-organisations and e-customers. It may be necessary to integrate the leadership system with the technology system.

## Restructuring

Is the corporate management term for the reorganising of the legal, ownership, operational, or other structures of a company to make it more profitable?

Other reasons; are - Change of ownership, or a response to a crisis or major change in the business, such as bankruptcy.

## Virtual teams

The leader must provide clear goals and communication rules, and there must be performance standards.

Teams of people who primarily interact electronically and be bought together, and meet face to face occasionally, particularly in large companies where people do not share the same office.

Not all projects are suitable for virtual managing, e.g., manufacturing, where reliance is upon a sequential or integrated work. Also, where there is a heavy exchange of information in real time or tasks have to go through a strict sequence of workers within a short time.

## Integrity leadership

Positive trait for a leader. It represents an honest, reliable, trustworthy person, with strong moral principles.

They shape the organisation to be integrity and respected by employees and the public.

Current Issues Impacting the roles of leaders.

Remote teams consist of a group of individuals who work across time, space, and often geographical boundaries.

Increasingly common and often poses new challenges for managers. Who needs to adjust accordingly? IT support is required, including teleconferencing, and training staff to use equipment is necessary.

A plan for managing performance needs to be in place, setting up objectives, and performance reviews. Paramount to the team's success will be the leader's skills for planning and managing performance, which needs to be in place, setting up objectives, and performance reviews. Training interventions can assist in motivating staff remotely.

Due to geographical disbursement developing a company culture can be challenging for remote workers. However, long -term success must have strong values and principles to give your company a unique character that staff can believe in.

Despite the difficulties in the distance, it is possible to grow a company when staff are around the world but will, as a leader, have to work a little harder at it.

A strong mission statement – short and memorable and philosophy
Hiring the right people – Candidates that are on the same wavelength

They will also need to be people who need minimum supervision.

Create a close-knit team

A team with shared values will always be more motivated than a loose collection of loners.

They like the freedom of their work but still like to be included in the team.

PowerPoint presentations of each other or sending a photograph of the homework area. Even a contest to guess whose work area it is.

Giving staff Independence

Letting them make their own decisions based on their knowledge of the company philosophy. The corporate principals will be cemented far more effectively, than if they just read them and have decisions made by them rather than just by the senior staff.

Don't micromanage - Instant messaging, phone calls, tracking computer time, logged in are all well and good, but the main question for managers may well be,

Are they getting the work done?
If the answer is yes, then leave them alone.

If the remote worker is the type of person who needs micromanaging, then the manager and recruitment team may have made a poor selection.

Recognise and reward

If one of your staff members does something that is a great example of your company culture, highlight this action.

Whether you mention it on a team call, write it on a company blog, or send a group email, recognizing and rewarding staff is a great way to boost morale and keep your company culture strong. And others are motivated and enthusiastic.

New technologies

Business mindsets are changing, so leaders must capitalise on the benefits that technologies can bring to the workplace. Managers should consider extending existing application investments to maximise the new way employees work.

Certain industries like marine and coastal environment agencies have benefited enormously and can report changes in fish and marine life through satellite mapping also from underwater cameras.

Smart grid technologies can assist with analyzing and testing technologies like car manufacturing. As they can grid the components on a construction area serviced by robots.

There has been an enormous advance in the London weather met centre, which has been able to report data more expediently and efficiently due to changes which could potentially save lives if there were to be an imminent storm or hurricane, for example

The economic climate in the global markets has also led to more competitive hiring and firing, As the economic activity has slowed down dramatically over the last few years. Some have argued it's created a "riskier" environment for small firms. According to research from the British chamber of commerce, the main causes were interest rate increases and a slowdown in gross domestic product.

Also, many managers and leaders are not investing inspending, which will adversely harm certain businesses exporting capabilities.

The higher small business tax rate has also dampened business confidence.

Resilient and adaptive strategies

Two related decision making strategies which might be particularly appealing when faced with high uncertainty. The first resilient strategy. This seeks to identify a range of possible future circumstances, and then choose approaches that work well across the spectrum of possibilities. Adaptive systems can be improved as more is learned as the future progresses.

Finally, changes in reporting is a term used when two or more previously separate companies are combined into one. Changes in reporting entities are shown as the restatement of all comparative statements, which includes the accounts, net income, and other comprehensive income.

A leader should use technology to ensure the new company runs smoother after the change. Many tools are effective, like Microsoft dynamic Ax, which will eliminate the need to install two different pieces of software to support reporting change.

Enterprise portals can be performed using SharePoint foundation or SharePoint server.

As can be seen from this chapter, several challenges arise for leaders. However, balanced with the information technology support now available and the ability in the global arena to pool resources and form partnerships I believe this will balance the equation and make things more equitable to manage.

## CHAPTER 2

# PROFESSIONAL SKILLS NEEDED
# FOR EFFECTIVE MANAGEMENT

*Different personal and professional skills needed for effective management. In this chapter I provide a case study of three successful well known leaders to provide comparison of skills and attributes for the different types.*
*– Sir Alan Sugar. Rupert Murdoch & Roman Abramovich*

S ir Alan Sugar has become famous for his contemporary program in the apprentice.

He is extremely popular on television but is now a British business magnate, media personality, and political advisor.

He started from humble origins in the East end of London. Sugar now has an estimated fortune of £770 million US dollars; it is 1.14 Billion and was ranked 89th in the Sunday times rich list 2011. Alan Michael Sugar, Baron Sugar, was born in 1947.

In 2007, he sold his remaining interest in the consumer electronics company Amstrad, his largest and best known business venture.

He is noted for his time as chairman of Tottenham Hotspur from 1991 to 2011. Also, for his appearances in the BBC television series the apprentice, which has been broadcast annually since 2005 and is based upon the popular US television show of the same name, featuring the American entrepreneur Donald Trump.

He was born into a Jewish family in a council flat in East London. He attended Northwold primary school and then Brooke house secondary school in upper Clapton, hackney. He made extra money by boiling and selling beetroot from a stall. After leaving school at 16, he worked briefly for the civil service as a statistician at the ministry of education.

He started selling aerials and electrical goods out of a van he had bought with his savings of £100. He now has a collection of classic Rolls Royce and Bentley motorcars. Sugar owns a Rolls Royce phantom with the number plate AMS1, which appears during all episodes of the apprentice.

A qualified pilot with 30 years of experience, Sir Sugar owns a Cirrus SR20 four set aircraft, based at staple ford airfield;

On 20th June 2009, he assumed the office of the House of Lords, joining the Labour government to advise on business and entrepreneurs.

He resigned as a Labour peer in 2015.

AMSTRAD

He founded it in 1968, the name being an acronym of his initials. Alan Michael sugar trading. Despite this acronym, sugar also trades under other business names.

The company began as a general exporter and wholesaler but soon specialised in consumer electronics.

By 1970, the first manufacturing venture was underway. He achieved lower production prices by using injection mo lding plastics for turntable covers, severely undercutting competitors.

His personal attributes are that he is a socialist and supports the Labour party movement, particularly to enable the economy to prosper through entrepreneurialism. He is very passionate about business and innovation.

He has invested his capital into the projects of the apprentice and supports the winner with a million-pound contract.

He provides mentoring and guidance to young people and has tried contributing to government policy on business issues.

His other qualities are anticipating the needs of people in advance of the consumer market. He did this with his Amstrad products for years. There was hardly anyone who did not own one during the 1980s as they were so popular.

His professional insight has helped the British economy to grow and has, I would say, contributed to the growth and stability of the country. Particularly as he has employed many younger and other skilled electronic professionals. He is commercially minded, and has a trusted circle of friends and an inner circle of staff. He has an autocratic leadership style that can often take criticism as a personal attack.

He has been influential in government and policy. He has three children and is a very supportive father and encourages them and is a role model.

There also seems to be a huge following of him, and he has inspired a generation of people into business and entrepreneurship. He is very passionate about all his projects, as can be seen when he was investing in Tottenham Hotspur. He certainly does not lack vision. He provides us with an example of the dedication and perseverance and strong will power required for successful leadership.

RUPORT MURDOCK

Australian American media mogul. Managing director of Australia news limited, inherited from his father in 1952.

He is the founder, chairman, and CEO of global media holding company News Corporation, the world's largest media conglomerate.

He was born Keith Rupert Murdock on the 11th of March 1931 in Melbourne, Victoria, Australia. He is a dual citizen of Australia and the United States of America. He was educated at Worcester College,

Oxford. He is the chairman and CEO of News Corporation and has a net worth of 8.3. Billion US.

He has six children and has been married three times.

In the 1950's and 1960's, he acquired various newspapers in Australia and New Zealand before expanding into the UK in 1969, taking over News of the world, followed closely by the sun.

He moved to New York in 1974 to expand into the US market and became a naturalised US citizen in 1985. In 1981, he bought the times, his first British broadsheet. In 1986, keen to adopt newer electronic publishing technologies, he consolidated his UK printing operations in Wapping, causing bitter industrial disputes. His news corporation acquired Twentieth Century Fox (1985), Harper Collins (1989), and Wall street journal (2007). He formed BskyB in 1990 and, during the 1990 s expanded into Asian networks and South American television. By 2000 Murdoch's news corporation owned over 800 companies in more than 50 countries with a net worth of over 5 billion.

In July 2011, Murdock faced allegations that his companies were hacking phones regularly of celebrities, royalty, and public citizens. He is currently having police and government investigations into bribery and corruption by the British government and FBI investigations in the United states.

He has English, Irish and Scottish ancestry.

Murdoch attended Geelong grammar school, where he had his first experience editing a publication, being co-editor of the students journal. He worked part-time at the Melbourne herald and was groomed by his father from an early age to take over the family business. His father was Keith Murdoch. (1885—1952). Robert Murdoch read philosophy, politics, and economics at Worcester College, Oxford University.

Where he supported the labour party. He managed oxford student publications limited, the publishing house of Cherwell newspapers. Murdoch completed a MA before working as a sub editor with the daily express for two years.

Following his father's death when he was 21, he returned from oxford to take charge of the family business News Limited. After purchasing the troubles Sunday Times in Perth, Australia in 1965 and acquired suburban and provincial newspapers throughout New South Wales, Queensland and Victoria over the years. This included the Sydney afternoon tabloid, known as the Daily Mirror.

He developed a pattern for his newspapers, increasing sports and scandal coverage and adopting eye-catching headlines. He expanded into New Zealand in 1964. Active also in politics in the national party of Australia. In 1968 Murdock entered the United Kingdom newspaper market by acquisition of the news of the world.

Followed in 1969 by the sun. Murdock turned the sun into a Tabloid format and reduced costs by using the same printing press for both newspapers.

During the 1980's and early 1990's, Murdoch's publications generally supported Britain's Prime Minister Margaret Thatcher. At the end of the Thatcher/Mayor era, Murdoch switched his support to the labour party and its leader Tony Blair.

In 1986, Murdoch introduced electronic production processes to his newspapers in Australia, Britain, and the United states. The greater degree of automation leads to significant reductions in the number of employees involved in the printing process. In England, the move roused the anger of the print unions, resulting in a long and often violent dispute that played out in Wapping.

The bitter dispute at wapping started with the dismissal of 6000 employees who had gone on strike resulting in street battles and demonstrations.

Many on the political left in Britain alleged the collusion of Margaret Thatcher's government with Murdoch in the wapping affair as a way of damaging the British trade union movement.

In 1987, the dismissed workers accepted a settlement of 60 million. He convinced British satellite broadcasting to accept a merger with sky television on his terms in 1990. They were quick to see the advantage of direct satellite broadcasting that did not require costly cable networks, and the merged company, BSkyB have dominated the British pay Television market ever since.

In the United states of America, in 1976, he purchased the New York post. He founded Fox broadcasting on 9th October 1986, which had great success with programmes such as The Simpsons and X files.

He also controls Fox movie studios and General motors, a car manufacturer worth 6 billion. Fox had huge success in the films Titanic and Avatar.

Murdoch's reputation and influence have been both positive and negative. He has been listed three times in the Time 100 as among the most influential people in the world. His net worth is 8.3. Billion dollars. He is the 38th richest person in the United States and the 106 richest person in the world. He is synonymous with unethical newspapers.

On writing this report, it was broadcast that Mr. Murdoch resigned from a string of directorships controlling his news corporations UK newspapers. Mr. Murdoch, 81, quit directorships at N group ltd, Newcorp investments, and Times newspaper holdings on Friday, 20th July 2012. Newscorp plans to split into two firms, separating its newspaper and book publishing interests from its now dominant television and film enterprises. Mr. Murdoch is expected to chair both businesses but to be chief executive only of the television and film side. News International has sought to play down the significance of the resignations.

Corporate house – cleaning

A spokesman said last week, Mr. Murdoch stepped down from several boards, many of them small subsidiary boards, both in the United Kingdom and the United States of America. This is nothing more than a corporate house cleaning exercise before the company split.

Media commentator Steve Hewlett told the BBC it was "no surprise" News Corporation was moving away from its newspaper investments because declining circulation in the industry and the phone hacking scandal had made for a nightmare. However, for

Murdoch to move away from these titles, in which he has invested 42 years of his life, is significant.

Some have commented "he is jettisoning those parts of the company that have become an embarrassment, and he's leaving those people that stuck with him for many decades behind", Said Labour M.P. Tom Watson.

In May 2012, the UK parliamentary media committee report stated, "he was not a fit and proper person to run a major international business.

In analysis and view of the Leveson inquiry, there is a strong temptation to read a great deal into Rupert Murdoch's resignation from the boards of three United Kingdom companies that control the Sun. The times and his other British newspapers. And given how much power and wealth these newspapers have conferred on him, the termination of his directorships of those UK companies is symbolic.

But the US parent company of all these newspapers says not too much should be read into the departures.

His spokesman described the resignations as a house – cleaning exercise in preparation for the already announced break up of two new corporation companies. And the point is that Rupert Murdock plans to be chairman of both these businesses, so although I may be a bit further removed from the famous British newspapers, they will continue to report to him .

When comparing him to Lord Alan Sugar

Both men have a driven and entrepreneurial attitude to business. Murdoch had a foot up as he inherited from his father.

He was born into a wealthy family and attended a private and world-renowned public university.

However, they are both leaders with an autocratic style. They like to be in control and are both extremely commercially minded.

They both know what the consumers want and need, and as Murdoch did by cutting his production costs at his newspapers, Sugar undercut his competitors at Amstrad.

They also have a close family around them, who are part of their inner circle, and both associate like the "spider's web" approach with powerful people in government and industry.

Both are interested in politics and active members of political parties. I would argue to further thier own political ambition and commercial domination of certain sectors. Due to his university degree, Murdoch also has economic skills that Sir Sugar buys in with more advisors. Murdoch has studied economics. Both men also rely upon their children for moral and business support.

Both men are very aware of presentation and ensure they are well dressed for their roles. Sugar is always suited and booted, as is Murdoch. They have a taste for the finer things in life and also both give to charity and support socialist good causes. However, they both live a "champagne" socialist lifestyle.

Obviously, due to the wealth disparity, Mr Murdoch's lifestyle exceeds that of Lord Sugar's. But they have similar autocratic characters.

## ROMAN ABRAMOVICH

Roman Arkadyevich Abramovich was born upon the 24th of October 1966 in Saratov. Russia, SFSR, Soviet union.

He has been married twice and also has a common-law partner. He has seven children from his first wife and two from his second wife. He also has children with his current partner.

He was a former politician and was an elected governor of Chukotka. He is of Eastern Slavic origin.

He is known in the United Kingdom as the owner of the Chelsea football club, an English premier league football team, and his wider involvement in European football.

Abramovich is currently the 9th richest person in Russia and the 68th richest person globally. According to the 2012 Forbes list, with an estimated fortune of US 12.1 Billion.

In Russia, he was an Oil tycoon and the main owner of the private investment company millhouse LLC.

He was born into a Jewish family of Latvian origins, Abramovich was orphaned as a child and was raised in his uncle's family living first in Ukhta, in the Komi republic, and then in Moscow. He attended regular state schools and was an average student.

Information on his university education is controversial. Some sources suggest he attended the Ukhta Industrial University, while others point to Moscow's Gubkin Russian state university . Both universities deny his attendance.

In Abramovich's official biography it states he graduated from the Moscow law academy in 2001, but rumours still circulate that he dropped out of college.

Some sources claim that this supposed law degree was completed in two years, whereas most law education institutions require at least four years of attendance.

*Business career*

Roman started his multi—billion dollar business during his army service, where he sold gasoline to some of the commissioned officers of his unit. After a brief stint in the soviet army, he married his first wife. He worked as a street trader and mechanic at a local factory.

At the peak of prestrocka, Abramovich sold imported rubber ducks from his Moscow apartment. Some sources suggest that these ducks were imported illegally, but no evidence exists. A 2000 pounds worth of ruby wedding present from Olga's parents was invested by Abramovich in the smuggling of black market goods or contraband to sell in Moscow in or around December 1987. Abramovich soon doubled, and then tripled, the investment, his confidence growing with each success in his smuggling business. Soon he progressed to making plastic dolls. It brought success almost immediately. Due to his business acumen, within a few years, his wealth spread from oil conglomerates to pig farms and also, he started investing in other businesses. Abramovich set up and liquidated at least 20 companies during the early 1990's, in sectors as diverse as tyre retreading and bodyguard recruitment.

From 1992—1995, he founded five companies that conducted resale, produced consumer goods, and acted as intermediaries, eventually specialising in trading oil and oil products. However, in 1992, he was arrested and sent to prison for theft of government property.

AVEKS—Komi sent a train containing 55 cisterns of diesel fuel, worth 3.8 million rubles, from the Ukuta oil refinery. Abramovich met the train in Moscow and resent the shipment to the Kaliningrad military base under a full agreement, but the fuel arrived in Riga.

Abramovich co—operated with the investigation, and the case was closed after the oil production factory was compensated by the diesel buyer, the Latvian - United States Company, chikora international.

In 1995, Abramovich and Boris Berezovsky, an associate of President Boris Yeltsin, acquired the controlling interest in the oil company subne t.

The deal was written within the controversial loans—for—shares program, with each partner paying £100 million for half of the company, below the stake stock market value of £150 million at the time, and rapidly turning it into billions. In hindsight, the company's fast-rising value led many observers to suggest that the real cost of the company should have been billions of dollars.

Abramovich later admitted in court that he paid huge bribes in billions to government officials and obtained protection from gangsters to acquire these and other assets, including alumin um assets, during the alumin um wars.

Thus, the main stages of Abramovich's financial career were Jan 1989—May 1991, as chairman of the cof co-op manufacturer of plastic toys May 1991—May 1992, and director of the ASK small enterprise, Moscow.

In 1992—1995 he set up five companies engaged in the production of consumer goods buying and selling. In 1996 he established another 10 firms. Stocks companies.

By 1996, at the age of 30, Abramovich had become so rich and politically well connected that he became close to President Boris

Yeltsin, and had moved into an apartment in the Kremlin at the invitation of the Yeltsin family. In 1999, and now a tycoon, he was elected governor of Russia's remote, far eastern province of Chukotka, and has since lavished 112 million pounds on charity to rebuild the impoverished nation.

He is a self made man, who was not only powerful and wealthy, but acutely aware of those who had done less well in the tumultuous 1990s when the Soviet Union fell. He was a member of the "family". A close circle around the then president, Boris Yeltsin, which included his daughter. In 1995, Sibneft was created by Boris Yeltsin's presidential decree. It was rumored that Abramovich was the chief of the organisation. He acquired a controlling interest in the giant Soviet oil company Sibneft The company was worth 2.7 billion at the time. Abramovich established several fly by night firms and, with his friend Boris Berezovsky used them to acquire stock in sibneft. As a result, the tycoon managed to pay for the company 25 times less than the market price. He bought for a total of 200 million, sibnefts is now worth seventy five times as much. This acquisition was under the controversial loans for shares initiated by thethen president Boris Yeltsin. After Sibneft, his next target was the alumin um industry. After privatization, the "aluminum wars" led to the murders of smelting plant managers, metal traders, and journalists as groups battled for control of the industry.

Abramovich famously emerged as the winner in the aluminum wars. Strangely after the oligarch (Abramovich) emerged at the top of the trade, the murders stopped.

Political career

In 1999 he was elected to the state Duma as representative for Chukatka Aut okrug. An impoverished region in the Russian Far East. He started the charity Pole of hope to help the people of Chukotka, especially children, and in December 2000, was elected governor of Chukotka, replacing Alexander Nazorov 2000 – 8.

He had some controversies in the aluminum wars, in which 100 people were believed to have been killed in gangland feuds over control of lucrative smelters. Numerous officials and executives were said to have lost their lives. Nevertheless, many of the allegations were unproven against him, and he has never been convicted of any crime in any world court.

He also faced allegations of loan fraud; along with other Russian politicians, he was alleged to have used International monetary funds as a personal slush fund. Although later, an audit by the IMF found that the funds had been used appropriately.

Berezovsky, his one time business partner, claims Roman harassed him with threats of intimidation to cheat him into selling his valuable shares at less than their true worth.

Bribes

In 2008, it was reported in the British newspaper the times that Abramorich admitted that he paid billions of dollars for political favours' and protection fees to obtain a big share of Russia oil and aluminum assets as was shown by court papers the times obtained through a source who disclosed it.

Yugraneft, an affiliate of Siber Energy, is seeking billions of dollars in damages in a lawsuit in London against Roman Abramovich and his investment company Millhouse capital, alleging that he was cheated out of its Russian assets.

The proceedings "involve" substantial claims to recover the proceeds of the diluted interest," said sibir energy, a company owned by the billionaire Shalva Chigrinisky. They were unsuccessful, and the high court found in Roman's favour earlier in the year. In July 2008, President Dmitri Medvedev, accepted Abramovich's latest request to resign as a governor of Chukotka, although his various charities in the region would continue. In his period of office, the average salaries increased from 100 Russian dragma to 500 per month. The regional government estimates that during his tenure Abramovich directed investment in the range of 2.5 billion to rebuild

Chukotka's crumbling housing, schools, hospitals, and infrastructure, much of the money coming from his pocket and through affiliated companies and his two foundations "pole of hope" and "Territora".

## Football

In 2003, Roman became the owner of the companies that control Chelsea football club in west London. He is present at almost every game Chelsea plays and shows visible emotion during matches, a sign of true dedication and genuine love for the sport and his club. He has also invested a lot of his wealth into the "purchase" of players. In Russia, he played a large role in bringing Guss Hiddink, the Russian coach, to the team. In addition to his involvement in professional football, Abramovich sponsors a foundation in Russia called the national football academy. The organisation sponsors youth sports programs. The charity has also constructed more than 50 football pitches around cities and towns in Russia. It also funds training programs for coaches, prints instruction material, renovates sports facilities, and takes top coaches and students to visit professional football clubs in England, Holland, and Spain.

Abramovich has a personal security team of over forty. In my view, it is like a "private army", making him one of the best-protected businessmen in the world. He sponsors Russian art and the Moscow house of photography. He owns millions of pounds of paintings, including Francis Bacon. He also has many luxury Yachts aircraft, and over sixty-five motor cars. Of which all are bullet and bomb proof.

## Comparison

His style of leadership is more delegative than the other two leaders that I have examined in this report. He works well when surrounded by trustworthy and solid staff. He has adopted this approach in both politics and football. However, he does share some traits of autocratic and defensive behaviour in certain instances, like the other two leaders.

He also surrounds himself in a bubble of the inner circle. He also has family close to him and enjoys the company of beautiful women and this is reflected in his wife's and fathering many children. He also has a caring side, as the other two have, and donates to charity as they do. However he has been more politically active than the other two when comparing their age to his. This may also be as a consequence of his background in Russia, and it may have been almost impossible not to be politically aware from a young age if living in the former Soviet – Union. He is richer than Lord Sugar but not Murdoch, but he still has some time to catch up due to his age. Since the Russian aggression against Ukraine, The United Kingdom has implemented sanctions, however, he has recently been able to sell Chelsea football clubs despite the financial restrictions placed on Russians internationally by governments.

Follow my example of volunteering at a justice peace group and analyse your leadership style.

In work groups, my leadership style, which is participative and sometimes defensive, could have the impact of following variables according to the particular dynamics of the group I am working with.

In my church group, where I was the chair and leader of the Justice and peace group. I would organise a program of activities. As I also took an active role this often meant that members did not allow me the space to prepare activities as I have engaged with them so much, I was seen as approachable.

The open – door policy that I operate has led to me being unable to explain I have tasks and duties as the leader of the group and need space and time to do this. Boundaries therefore must be put in place which can be hard to enforce.

This is due to the requirement for me as the leader to be friendly and genuine, as no one likes to be a fake. I want to enable the newcomers and members of the church not to resist accepting people into their circle of trust.

So I take a real interest in them and ask a lot of non – threatening questions.

We mainly then have to move into the next stage of discussing personal issues and their opinions and feelings, as that is needed for me to produce a work program for the justice and peace year.

In the Albert Mehrabian theory, I have to create effective relationships on face-face communication, as those that have joined the group are already trusting. It's not a hurdle, but for those who have not joined I need to establish a mutuality of purpose and connect with those who have not joined. Due to the faith background of most of them they are open to issues to do with justice and inequalities, as Jesus' story has a lot of that involved!

It is not about winning a popularity contest, as the group I lead does compete with other groups as people have different interests. So for the relationship to develop. I am reliable, they know that I will be there when I say, and that there will be food, drinks, and music provided. Some church members have a closed mind and it can find it difficult to remain enthusiastic when I engage with anything other than traditional forms of work.

# CHAPTER 3

# MANAGEMENT THEORIES

In linking my previous chapter on management styles, it is useful to now consider theories such as Adair, Peters, Kanter, and Mitzberg.

Adair is linked with this team building, and how he relates the tasks with the people and the resources. Adair in 1934. One of Britain's foremost authorities on leadership before him was the "great man theory". Which was one charismatic individual who used their personal power and rhetoric to mobilise a group? Adair approached leadership from a more practical, simple angle; by describing what leaders must do and the actions they need to take.

1. Achieve the task
2. Build and maintain the team
3. Develop the individual

Adair's theory shows that leadership can be taught and is a transferable skill. The three circles in Adair's model overlap because;

1. The task needs a team because one person alone cannot accomplish it.
2. If the team's needs are not met, the task will suffer, and the individuals will not be satisfied.

3. If the individual needs are not met, the team will suffer and performance of the task will be impaired.

Leadership functions

Adair lists eight functions required to achieve success. These need to be constantly developed and homes to ensure success.

Defining the task using SMART goals

1. Specific. Measurable, achievable, realistic, and time constrained.
2. Planning an open - minded, positive, and creative search for alternatives. Contingencies should be planned for, and plans should be tested.
3. Briefing Team briefings by the leader are a basic function and essential to create the right atmosphere, fostering teamwork, and motivating each individual.
4. Controlling leaders need self-control, good control systems in place, and effective delegation and monitoring skills in order to get maximum resources.
5. Evaluating assess consequences, evaluate performance, appraise and train individuals.
6. Motivating, Adair identifies eight basic rules for inspiring people. In his book effective motivation Guildford: Talbot Adair press, 1987. Adair also created the 50; 50 rule which states that 50% of motivation comes from within a person and 50% from his or her environment and particularly the leadership they encounter.
7. Organising Good leaders must be able to organise themselves, their team, and their organisation.
8. Setting an example. The best leaders naturally set a good example. If effort needs to be made, it will slip, and a bad example is noticed more than a good example.

Motivating your team

The eight rules for motivating people

1.  Be motivated yourself
2.  Select motivated people
3.  Treat each person as an individual
4.  Set realistic but challenging targets
5.  Understand that progress itself motivates
6.  Create a motivating environment
7.  Provide relevant rewards
8.  Recognise success

John Adair's work aligns with motivational theorists such as Maslow, McGregor, and Herzberg. He empathises with the need for the development of the team and team building. This can be achieved through team building events and using theories like Belbin. Where Adair identifies the need, Belbin provides one of the tools.

Tom Peters is known for his excellence theories of the 1970's and as a motivational speaker.

Theories of the 1970's and as a motivational speaker. An American writer on business and management practices. Includes the "seven S framework" strategy, structure and systems (hard s's) staff style, shared values, and skills (soft s's). These tips are the means for a company to analyse itself.

Tom Peters is considered one of the gurus of business management and the most influential business theorist of our time. Over time he has added, modified, and continually grown his original theory.

He provided huge lengthy lists of what leadership is.

For him, leadership is a bunch of paradoxes, (like much else); it's both simple and complex, digging deep and soaring high, all about the people yet potentially lonely.

Here is a synopsis of Peter's style leadership to do – list.

1. Uncertainty is here to stay. You can be certain of that: Be prepared to say, "I don't know".
2. Be a dealer to keep an eye out for grand possibilities. Inspire others by throwing down a great challenge.
3. Do something! Become an action figure. Life's too short of striving to be right the first time. Get on with it. Behave like a venture capitalist. Take lots of risks and make lots of bets. Keep churning your "portfolio" of interesting people and projects.
4. Accept mistakes as the price of greatness.
5. Bring people together. Create the shortest distance between talented people. Don't just order them because "ordering" change wastes time.
6. Succession plan. Mentor, mentor, mentor. Encourage and cultivate the next generation of leaders.
7. Find the "freaks," for they shall inherit the earth!
8. Deliver a forum for the "freaks" to showcase their groovy stuff.
9. Protect them from the doom - mongers and naysayers.
10. Cut from your organisation those who don't measure up ruthlessly and charitably.
11. Promote the wackiest, youngest, coolest "freaks"! Often.
12. Make finding incredible talent your number one priority to actively and aggressively seek out the very best. Pay well for the very best.
13. Leadership is a confidence game. Act the part.
14. Get rid of all the clutter that undermines your security of focus. Create a to do list and add to it frequently.
15. Take a break – chill out. Let your projects mature. Don't try to control the "fruits of your boss's work".
16. Love, laugh. Smile and express your passion for what you do.

In the analysis, I do feel that my justice and peace style, the 50:50 rule of Adair concerning motivation, applies to my style and due to the leaders role models I have encountered in higher education colleges and universities, which consisted of all middle and upper-class tutors.

With Peter's theory, I have adopted a structure and strategy to promote justice and peace in other parts of the parish, and we have systems provided by the priest and bishop to do this. These are called the (hard s's). Another trait I have in my style from the theory is hope and keeping an eye out for grand possibilities. This is due to the faith background of the charity. My mother always taught me to accept my mistakes and keep trying. She would say, "If, at first, you don't succeed, try try again".

My leadership style involves being passionate about what I do and loving it, laughing, and smiling. However, sometimes if I don't have the structure, logistical, and operational support, my health can diminish, making the momentum difficult for the project. As no one can do much and function at a peak level if they are burned out and under stress.

## KANTER 1977

The theory recognizes that there are critical business relationships that cannot be confronted by formal systems but require a dense web of interpersonal connections. "Collaborative Advantage" In her 1994, Harvard business school review article. "Collaborative needs a different kind of leadership, it needs leaders who can safeguard the process, facilitate interaction and patiently deal with high levels of frustration". Collaboration is defined as a purposeful relationship in which all parties strategically choose to operate to accomplish a shared "outcome". The theory feels that the collaborative leader is;

- someone who has accepted the responsibility for building or helping to ensure the success of a heterogeneous team to accomplish a shared purpose.

Your tools are (1) The purposeful exercise of your behaviour, communication, and organisational resources to affect another person's perspective, beliefs, and behaviours. Generally, a collaborative partner. To influence that person's relationship with you and your collaborative enterprise, and (2) The structure and climate of an environment that supports the collaborative relationship.

In the church Justice and peace, we have a head commission based in the UK, which is funded by the diocese of Westminster.

The justice and peace commission's direction for the work program is from the Holy Father, the pope, who appointed a president assistant secretary, and under secretary that he named for a certain period of years under papal decree The primary purpose is to engage in "action oriented studies" for the international promotion of Justice, peace, and human rights.

To this end, it cooperates with various religious institute advocacy groups, scholarly ecumenical, and international organisations.

The main three areas of justice and peace work is;

1. Social justice, work and employment trade justice international development and ethical practice.
2. Peace, working towards nuclear disarmament and the arms trade and international security and violence and its various and ever changing forms, e.g., terrorism and extreme nationalism.
3. Human rights Pope John Paul gave this more of a larger role in the mission of justice and peace consequently the justice and peace work focuses on the dignity of the human person, and is the foundation and promotion of his and her defence of their inalienable rights. The council shows concern for human rights violations, supports cases and makes submissions and recommendations to the executive of justice and peace and to international institutions that promote human dignity.

I am currently for the last year in the church promoting fair- trade and economic justice for farmers and those in developing countries whose produce is exploited.

We have to work collaboratively with "fair-trade," "cafod," and "tradecraft" and other organisations in the collaborative enterprise that supports the collaborative relationship that Kanter refers to. As we have a shared purpose. This is how the theory has impacted on my style of leadership.

In the model of MINTZBERG Professor Henry Mitzberg is an internationally renowned academic and author on business and management. He has lectured in management studies since 1968. He advocates "action learning" and students learning "insights" from their problems and experiences. He is heavily critical of graduate management schools, which he feels over zealously tries to make management science, which he feels damages the discipline of management.

Theory on organisational forms

The organisational configurations framework of Mitzberg is a model that describes six valid organisational configurations (originally only five, the sixth one was added later).

1. Simple structure characteristic of entrepreneurial organisation.
2. Machine bureaucracy
3. Professional bureaucracy
4. Diversified form
5. Advocacy or innovative organisation
6. Missionary organisation

Regarding the coordination between different tasks, Mitzberg defines the following mechanisms.

1. Mutual adjustment, which achieves coordination by the simple process of informal communication.
2. Direct supervision is achieved by having one person issue orders or instructions to several others whose work interrelates. When a boss tells others what is to be done, one step at a time.

3. Standardardization of work processes, which achieves co-ordination by specifying the work processes of people carrying out interrelated tasks; those standards usually being developing in the techno structure due to be carried out in the operational core, as in the case of the work instructions that come out of time and motion studies.

4. Standardisation of outputs, which achieves co-ordination by specifying the results of different work. Again usually developed in the technostructure, as in a financial plan that specifies performance targets or specifications that outline the dimensions of a product to be produced.

5. Standardisation of skills, as well as knowledge, in which the related training workers coordinate different work, as in medical specialists. Say a surgeon and anesthetist in an operating room respond almost automatically to each other standardised procedures.

6. Standardisation of norms, in which it is the norms infusing the work that is controlled, usually for the entire organisation, so that everyone functions according to the same set of beliefs as in religious order.

According to the organisational configurations model of Mitzberg each organisation can consist of a maximum of six basic parts.

1. Strategic apex (top management)
2. Middle line (Middle management)
3. Operating core (operations, operational processes)
4. Technostructure (the analysis that designs systems, processes, etc.)
5. Support staff (support outside of operating workflows)
6. Ideology (Halo of beliefs and traditions, norms, values, cultures)

Concerning the role that I play at the commission, this is a theory that we use in a minor way. Specifically, when we look at standardisation of skills and norms, as the members are also catholic and some are trained in a standardised way as with the religious norms, that infuse the work, and that is controlled by the entire organisation, so that we all function to the same set of beliefs.

I will examine and analyse the relationship between management and leadership and the difference between leadership and management in terms of behaviour using theorists such as Adair, Bennis, Covey, and Drucker.

## *Differentiation between management and leadership styles in given situations*

The biggest difference between managers and leaders is how they motivate the people they work with. I believe modern leadership demands finding the right balance between leadership and management in given situations. I will provide some examples of this later on in the chapter. The strengths and weaknesses all have to be considered by the individual manager or leader; the second question is what are the needs of the situation.

What is required is the ability to adapt your style to the given situations to achieve maximum effectiveness. If you lead in a manner that is solely in line with your preferred leadership style, then you will fail to be effective. If you only try to adapt to the situation, you will suffer from executive burnout. Understanding those competing demands is an important step towards finding the right balance between success and personal fulfillment.

I have set out some styles that may be used depending on the situation;

Explanation of the relationship between management & leadership

DEFINITIONS OF MANAGEMENT

Leadership is one of the many assets a successful manager must possess. Care must be taken in distinguishing between the two concepts. The main aim of the manager is to maximise the output of the organisation through the practice of implementation. To achieve this manager must undertake the following functions;

Planning, coordinating, controlling, organising, and directing. Leadership is just one of the important components of the directing function. A manager cannot just be a leader; he also needs formal authority to be effective.

In some circumstances, leadership is not required. For example, self–motivated groups may not require a single leader and may find leaders dominating. The fact that a leader is not always required is a sure sign that leadership is just an asset and is not essential.

Differences in perspectives

Managers think incrementally, while leaders think radically. Managers do the right thing. This means that managers prefer things by the book and follow company policy, while leaders follow their own intuition, which may in turn be of more benefit to the company. A leader is more emotional than a manager. "Men are governed by their emotions rather than their intelligence." *John Fenton 101 ways to improve your business* pg 113 1990. This quotation illustrates why teams choose to follow leaders. Members of staff, with specific talents who lead the group in a certain direction. When a natural leader emerges in a group containing a manager, conflict may arise if they have different views. When the managers see the group looking towards someone else for leadership, they may feel their authority is being questioned.

Groups are often more loyal to a leader than a manager. This loyalty is created by the leader taking responsibility in the area such as:

Taking the blame when things go wrong.
Celebrating group achievements.
Giving credit where it's due.

The leader must highlight the successes within a team using charts or graphs, with little presentations and fun ideas. They are observant and sensitive people. They know their team and develop confidence within it.

In my research, I would summarise a leader as someone who people naturally follow through with their own choice, whereas a manager must be obeyed. A manager may only have obtained his position through time and loyalty given to the company, not due to his leadership qualities. Leaders may have no organisational skills, but their vision unites people behind them. Management usually consists of people who are experienced in their fields and who have worked their way up the company. A manager knows how each layer of the system works and may possess good technical knowledge. A leader can be a new arrival who has bold, fresh, new ideas but might not have experience or industry wisdom. Managing and leading are two different ways of organising people. The manager uses a formal, rational method, while the leader uses passion and stirs emotions.

William Wallace is one excellent example of a brilliant leader but could never be thought of as the manager of the scots!

## Intimacy: Getting Close

Personal conversation flourishes so that the participants stay close to each other, figuratively and literally. Organisational conversation, similarly, requires leaders to minimise the distances—institutional, attitudinal, and sometimes spatial—that typically separate them from their employees. Where conversational intimacy prevails, those with decision-making authority seek and earn the trust (and hence the careful attention) of those who work under that authority. They cultivate the art of listening to people at all levels of the organisation and learning to speak with employees directly and authentically. Physical proximity between leaders and employees isn't always feasible. Nor is it essential. What *is* vital is mental or emotional proximity. Conversationally adept leaders step down from their corporate perches and then step up to the challenge of communicating personally and transparently with their people.

This intimacy distinguishes organisational conversation from long-standard forms of corporate communication. It shifts the focus from a top-down distribution of information to a bottom-up exchange of ideas. It's less corporate in tone and more casual. And it's less about issuing and taking orders than asking and answering questions.

Conversational intimacy can manifest in various ways—gaining trust, listening well, and getting personal.

**Gaining trust.** Where there is no trust, there can be no intimacy. For all practical purposes, the reverse is true as well. No one will dive into a heartfelt exchange of views with someone who seems to have a hidden agenda or a hostile manner. Any discussion between two people will be rewarding and substantive only to the extent that each person can take the other at face value.

## Leadership behaviours and development of leadership style and skills

Leadership skills are based on leadership behaviour. Skills alone do not make leaders - style and behaviour do. If you are interested in leadership training and development - start with leadership behaviour.

The growing awareness and demand for idealist principles in leadership are increasing the emphasis (in terms of leadership characteristics) on business ethics, corporate responsibility, emotional maturity, personal integrity, and what is popularly now known as the 'triple bottom line' (abbreviated to TBL or 3BL, representing 'profit, people, planet').

For many people (staff, customers, suppliers, investors, commentators, visionaries, etc.), these are becoming the most significant areas of attitude/behaviour/appreciation required in modern business and organisational leaders.

3BL (triple bottom line - profit, people, planet) also provides an excellent multi-dimensional framework for explaining, developing, and assessing leadership potential and capability and also links strongly with psychology aspects if, for instance, psychometrics (personality testing) features in leadership selection and development methods: each of us is more naturally inclined to one or the other (profit, people, planet) by our personality, which can be referenced to Jung, Myers Briggs,

Much debate persists as to the validity of "triplr bottom line accounting" since standards and measures are some way from being clearly defined and agreed upon, but this does not reduce the relevance of the concept, nor the growing public awareness of it, which effectively and continuously re-shapes markets and therefore corporate behaiour.

Accordingly, leaders must understand and respond to such huge attitudinal trends and whether they can be reliably accounted for.

Adaptability and vision - as might be demonstrated via project development scenarios or tasks - especially involving modern communications and knowledge technologies - are also critical for certain leadership roles, and provide unlimited scope for leadership development processes, methods, and activities.

Cultural diversity is another topical and relevant area requiring leadership involvement, if not mastery. Large organisations must recognise that the marketplace, in terms of staff, customers and suppliers, is truly global now, and leaders must be able to function, appreciate and adapt to all aspects of cultural diversification. A leader who fails to relate culturally well and widely, and openly inevitably condemns the entire organisation to adopt the same narrow focus and bias exhibited by the leader.

Remember that different leadership jobs (and chairman) require different types of leaders - Churchill was fine for war but not good for peacetime rebuilding. There's a big difference between the short-term return on investment versus long-term change. Each warrants a different type of leadership style, and very few leaders can adapt from one to the other. (Again, see the personality styles section: short-term results and profit require strong Jungian 'thinking' orientation or frontal left brain dominance, whereas long-term vision and change require 'intuition' orientation or frontal right brain dominance).

If it's unclear already, leadership is, without a doubt, mostly about behaviour, especially towards others. People who strive for these things generally come to be regarded and respected as a leader by their people:

Integrity - is the most important requirement; without it, everything else is for nothing.

Having an effective appreciation and approach towards corporate responsibility (Triple Bottom Line, Fair Trade, etc, so that the need to make a profit is balanced with wider social and environmental responsibilities.

Being very grown-up - never getting emotionally negative with people - no shouting or ranting, even if you feel very upset or angry.

Leading by example - always be seen to be working harder and more determinedly than anyone else.

Helping alongside your people when they need it.
Fairness - treating everyone equally and on merit.
Being firm and clear in dealing with bad or unethical behaviour.

Listening to and understanding people and showing them that you understand (this doesn't mean you have to agree with everyone - understanding is different from agreeing).

Always taking responsibility and blame for your people's mistakes.
Always giving your people credit for your successes. Never self-promoting.
Backing up and supporting your people.

Being decisive - even if the decision is to delegate or do nothing if appropriate - but be seen to be making fair and balanced decisions.

Asking for people's views but remaining neutral and objective.

Be honest but sensitive in how you give bad news or criticism.

Always doing what you say you will do - keeping your promises.

Working hard to become an expert at what you do technically and understanding your people's technical abilities and challenges.

Encourage your people to grow, learn, and take on as much as they want to at a pace they can handle.

Always accentuating the positive (say 'does it like this,' not 'don't do it like that').

Smiling and encouraging others to be happy and enjoy themselves.

Relaxing - breaking down the barriers and the leadership awe - and giving your people and yourself time to get to know and respect each other.

Taking notes and keeping good records.

Planning and prioritising.

Managing your time well and helping others to do so too.

Involving your people in your thinking and especially in managing change.

Reading good books, and taking advice from good people, help develop your understanding of yourself, particularly of other people's weaknesses (some of the best books for leadership are not about business at all - they are about people who triumph over adversity).

Achieve the company tasks and objectives while maintaining your integrity, the trust of your people, are balancing the corporate aims with the needs of the world beyond.

## Adair Adair's model of Leadership Functions

## The Blake Mouton Managerial Grid (Blake & Mouton, 1964)

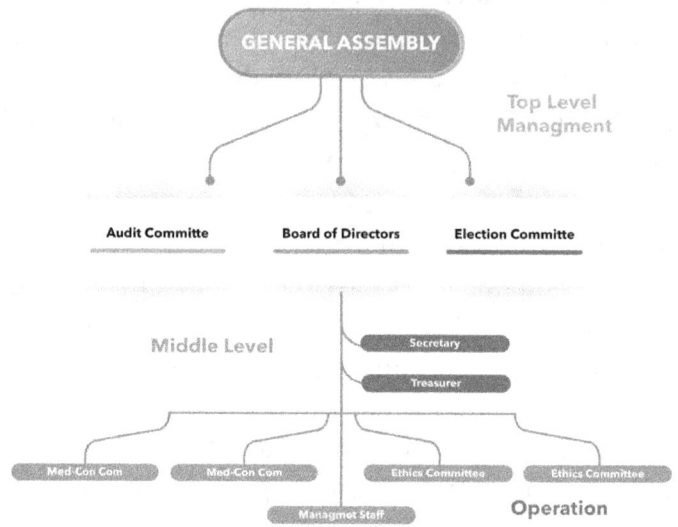

Adair, J, Leadership Skills, Chartered Institute of Personnel Development, London, 1997.

A business tool that describes the three core roles of leadership as overlapping and interdependent spheres. The model´s 3 spheres are: achieving the task, building and maintaining the team, and developing the individual. These areas are mutually dependent and equal. In addition to these three roles, Adair identified eight vital leadership functions or behaviour types. These functions are: defining the task, planning, and briefing, controlling, evaluating, motivating, organising, and providing examples.

### Core Roles

Achieving the task depends not only on a clear plan but also on individuals being motivated and the group pulling together. The group can only effectively operate if the task is achievable and well-defined and the individuals are motivated. The individuals' development and motivation require the task to be clear and achievable and the group to be supportive and effective. In this sense, each role needs to function effectively so that the other two areas are satisfied. To achieve this equilibrium, the leader must continually perform the eight leadership functions:

Defining the task: This sets a clear objective allowing the group and the individual to have a collective goal.

Planning: Both leader and team need to be aware of timescales and responsibilities to achieve cohesion, efficiency, and clarity of procedure.

Briefing: Giving and receiving information and summarising ideas. This benefits individuals through a sense of inclusion and teams by sharing information as a sign of democracy.

Controlling: The leader needs to exercise self-control and implement effective control systems for the group and individuals. This ensures standards are met to achieve the task and builds confidence in the leadership capabilities of the individuals and teams.

Evaluating: Continual evaluation of individual and group performance is essential for developing and maintaining standards and skills.

Motivating: Leaders can benefit teams and individuals by reconciling disagreements and providing encouragement through setting realistic targets and communication feedback.

Organising: Efficient allocation of people, time, and resources benefit the task by making it more achievable for individuals and teams by providing a clear action plan.

Providing examples: Leading by example builds credibility with teams and individuals and helps build motivation and efficiency in individuals.

The model demonstrates the unity of leadership and shows how acting on any one of the eight functions or behaviours by the leader has a knock-on effect across the three core areas. The tool provides an integrated approach to leadership and is relevant for all team members and leaders.

Management and leadership style that impact upon the achievements of organisational objectives.

- **Autocratic:** The leader takes the decisions and announces them, expecting subordinates to carry them out without question (the *Telling* style).
- **Persuasive:** At this point on the scale, the leader also takes all the decisions for the group without discussion or consultation but believes that people will be better motivated if they are persuaded that the decisions are good ones. They do a lot of explaining and 'selling' to overcome any possible resistance to what they want to do. The leader also puts a lot of energy into creating enthusiasm for the goals they have set for the group (the *Selling* style).
- **Consultative:** In this style, the leader confers with the group members before making decisions and, in fact, considers their advice and their feelings when framing decisions. They may not always accept the subordinates' advice, but they are likely to feel that they can have some influence. Under this leadership style, the decision and the full responsibility for it remain with the leader. Still, the degree of involvement by subordinates in decision taking is much greater than in telling or selling styles (the *Consulting* style).
- **Democratic:** Using this style, leaders would characteristically lay the problem before their subordinates and invite discussion. The leader's role is that of the conference leader, or chair, rather than that of the decision-maker. They will allow the decision to emerge out of the process of group discussion instead of imposing it on the group as its boss (the *Joining* style).

Influences of the style, e.g., culture of organisation, beliefs, and values of manager/leader.

Culture refers to the distinctive collective mental programming of values and beliefs within society. (Hofstede, 1980).

National culture can be compared using four dimensions: collectivism – individualism, power distance, uncertainty avoidance, and masculinity–femininity. (Hofstede, 1980).

National cultures can be compared using four dimensions: collectivism – individualism, power distance, uncertainty avoidance, and masculinity–femininity (Hofstede, 1980).

E.gIndian culture may differ from America in that Indian culture has a higher power distance and lower individualism than American culture (Agrawel, 1993).

Collectivism – individualism is the degree to which individuals are more interested in group welfare vs. self-welfare.

Power distance is the degree to which those with less power accept the authority of those with more power. Each culture has unique beliefs, values systems, attitudes, and behaviours that determine managerial behaviour. (Chakraborty, 1991). Therefore, it follows that employees from different national cultures have learned and experienced different managerial practices, and each culture must be explored within its perimeters'.

Managerial practices that work effectively in one culture often work poorly in others. They alert global managers to the danger of assuming that effective management practice is universal. This, in my opinion, means that there will need to be an adaptation of management practices to suit the national cultures in which they operate to achieve a high level of managerial performance.

Comparison of western developed measures, such as Machiavellianism, locus of control, intolerance of ambiguity, and dogmatism. Within the eastern developed Chinese value survey found Confucian, dynamism, human-heartedness, integration, and moral discipline. Culture and the business environment interact to create a unique set of managerial values in different countries. Ralston et al. (1992)

Understanding differences in value and value dimensions has a profound impact on effective cross–cultural management.

Earley & Erz (1997). Effectively argue in their book that a direct relationship between culture and managerial beliefs, practices, and cultural value shapes the meaning of varied aspects of the workplace. Managerial practices that work effectively in one culture often work poorly in others. They alert global managers to the danger of assuming that effective management practices are universal.

Emotional leadership styles, e.g., Goleman's six styles. Hay and McBer's Goleman's six styles are:

1. Coercive style of leadership. A dominant "macho" leadership. These types can be useful in emergencies and severe situations. They tend to disempower subordinates, but they can also disillusion them.
2. The authoritative style of leadership is "the visionary." Focuses on the goal or vision of the future and inspires others to follow. These characters are useful in change and reform or when a new direction is required or a classification of the goals to be achieved.
3. An affiliative style, "the people's person." Focuses on people, team building, bonding, and forging alliances. Useful in creating teams or for healing a dysfunctional relationship.
4. A democratic style, "the listener." They are useful to adopt when attempting to involve a wide range of people in decision-making or building a consensus.
5. With the pacesetting style "the superman/superwoman." Here the leader sets an example by working to extremely high-performance standards. These leaders can be useful in raising the stakes when a competent and motivated team is working well.
6. The coaching style is "The nurturer." They focus on helping to improve people's strengths, which is especially useful in building skills to develop managers and future leaders.

In my considered opinion of the Golemans' six styles of leadership models, a complete leader would use a combination of all of these. I would also go further as to say that a shift in application depending on the goal is advisable to lead a team or project successfully.

Emotional competence inventory Dulewicz and Higgs leadership dimensions.

### 7.1.1 Higgs Report on Non-Executive Directors

The most influential recent report on corporate governance in the UK is the Higgs report on non-executive directors (January 2003). This report sets out the role of non-executive directors concerning the board and chairman. The text below is edited from the full report.

**Role of the Board**

It is argued that the role and the effectiveness of the non-executive director need to be considered in the context of the board as a whole. The role of the board

- The board is collectively responsible for promoting the company's success by directing and supervising the company's affairs.
- The board's role is to provide entrepreneurial leadership of the company within a framework of prudent and effective controls which enable risk to be assessed and managed.
- The board should set the company's strategic aims, ensure the necessary financial and human resources are in place to meet its objectives and review management performance.
- The board should set the company's values and standards and ensure that its obligations to its shareholders and others are understood and met.

Professor Victor Dulewicz, Ph.D., created a Dulewicz leadership dimension questionnaire (LDQ). He developed it following extensive research into the behaviour and performance of senior managers and directors. The research showed findings that emotional intelligence is even more important than IQ in predicting an individual's potential and that emotional intelligence can be developed. (1993)

Professor Dulewicz is currently conducting research into corporate leadership and managers and change.

### 5.2.8 National College for School Leadership – Hay McBer Model

In 1999 the NCSL commissioned Hay McBer to research leadership in schools. This research led to the development of a model of school leadership, which formed the basis of further discussion. The NCSL now seems to be moving away from this approach towards an integrated leadership development framework.

The 17 school leadership qualities in the Hay McBer Model are as follows:

1. Analytical Thinking
2. Challenge and Support
3. Confidence
4. Developing Potential
5. Drive for Improvement
6. Holding People Accountable
7. Impact and Influence
8. Information Seeking
9. Initiative
10. Integrity
11. Personal Convictions
12. Respect for Others
13. Strategic Thinking
14. Team working
15. Transformational Leadership
16. Understanding the Environment
17. Understanding Others

## The Blake Mouton Managerial Grid (Blake & Mouton, 1964)

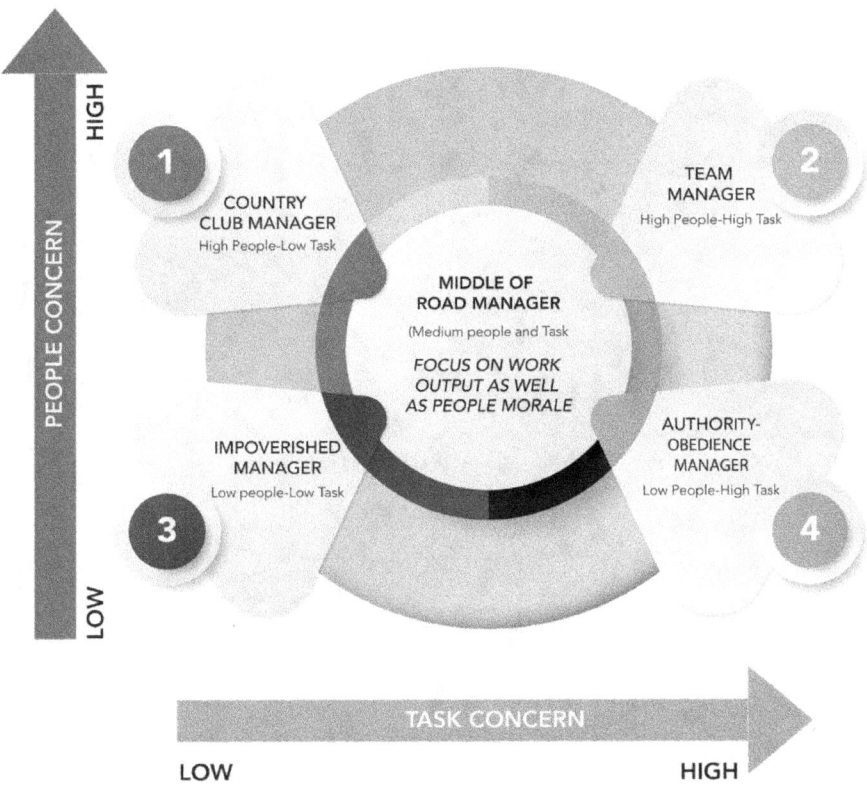

Copyright Catherine Tuitt MBE LLB hons

# CHAPTER 4

# LEARNING, WHICH STYLE ARE YOUR EMPLOYEES OR YOU?

There are several learning styles that most individuals will fall within. These depend on the person and their development, and generally, there may be two that cover the behaviour and way they are cognitively able to process information and learn.

I will seek to cover the main ones

Kolb's
Fleming's
VARK/VAK model
Assessment of my learning style

The Importance of continual self-development

A skills audit reviews your existing skills against the skills you need both now and in the future. It can help you to identify your existing skills, identify what skills you may need to carry out your existing voluntary work and role more effectively and to plan, develop and improve the skills and knowledge required for your future career.

Carrying out a skills audit is a five stage process.

## STAGE 1 - EXISTING SKILLS AND KNOWLEDGE IDENTIFICATION

First, you write down, as a bullet point list, the knowledge, and skills that you consider important for your current voluntary work. You may find it useful to refer to the section 'How are skills learnt' to do this and to refer to your 'job description' (including your voluntary/charity work).

## Stage 2 - Future Skills and Knowledge Identification

Next, write down as a bullet point list the knowledge and skills that you consider important for your future career.

Each list should comprise roughly between fifteen to twenty bullet points.

## STAGE 3 - RATING YOUR ABILITY

Once you have produced your lists, you need to rate your current ability against each one. This may be done via a 3-point rating of strong, weak, and somewhere in-between, or you may find it more useful to use a five - point scale such as the one below.

1. = No current knowledge or skill (no current competency),
2. = Some awareness but not sufficiently competent to use it,
3. = Familiar with and able to use the knowledge or skill (some competency),
4. = Proficient in the knowledge or skill and able to show others how to use it (high level of competency),
5. = Expert with high skill and comprehensive knowledge (fully competent).

Stage 4 - Review Your Ability Ratings

Next, ask a friend, supervisor, or tutor, in this case, Steve Burnham of smart training, to review your list and give you feedback. Try to ensure that you choose someone honest and not afraid to tell you the truth. If they are unwilling, there is no point in asking a close friend to be honest for fear that they may hurt your feelings by telling you that you are possibly not as good as you think.

Stage 5 - Your Future Development

The final stage is simply using the information to concentrate on developing the skill and knowledge areas where you have a low score or have identified that you are not fully competent.

A more advanced method of carrying out a skills audit is to produce three bullet point lists:

1.  Behavioural skills

    These transerable personal and interpersonal skills are necessary for almost every career. These are typically the skills of:

    Communication, working with and relating to others, problem solving communication skills, ITC skills, mathematical skills, self-management and development, time management, managing tasks, time management, communicating clearly and effectively, and applying initiative.

2.  Technical knowledge and skills

    These are specific to the technical/ professional area(s) in which you work. For example: if you are doing voluntary work in a school there may be specific knowledge you may need in order to work with children, or, if you know that your chosen career will be as a counsellor then you will identify that you need to develop specific counselling skills.

3.  Other knowledge and skills

Those which do not appear on either of the other two lists. They may relate specifically to the area that you do your voluntary work in and may include particular methods and procedures you use or may relate to the position that you occupy and role you carry out. In my case, I do many tasks and duties due to the role I held in the past at my church and in the archdiocese.

Preliminary knowledge & skills audit

| Knowledge and skills which I consider to be important for my current voluntary activity | Your Ability Rating (1-5) or strong/weak / somewhere in between |
| --- | --- |
|  |  |
| Knowledge and skills which I consider to be important for my future career | Your Ability Rating (1-5) or strong/weak / somewhere in between |
|  |  |

There is a range of skills that are not only significant to employment from both the perspective of an employer and employee. But also to your personal development and employability.

This skills audit helps me to identify my strengths, weaknesses, and areas for development within various skills areas.

If you find where you need support, there is a range of provisions available at the University to help you. Further information can be found at the end of the document.

## *PERSONAL SWOT ANALYSIS*

A range of skills is not only significant to learning in higher education and academic achievement but also to personal development and employability.

This skills audit will help me to identify my strengths, weaknesses and areas for development within opportunities in various skills areas. Also the potential threats.

My desired job role as a lawyer will be used as a benchmark. To see if I meet the competencies required in order to fulfill organisational objectives.

**How to complete the audit**

Read the SKILLS AREA, place a tick in the column that best suits your ability, and then decide the priority for YOU in developing this skill in the final column.

I tried to be as realistic and truthful as possible.

| SKILLS AREA | I CAN DO THIS WELL | OK, BUT I NEED MORE PRACTICE | I CAN'T DO THIS | PRIORITY DEVELOPMENT OF THIS SKILL 1 = very important, 2 = quite important, 3 = not important |
|---|---|---|---|---|
| ORGANISATION OF LEARNING | | | | |
| I have strategies to help me to plan and manage my time | | | | |
| I can effectively prioritise my tasks and activities | | | | |
| I can work to deadlines | | | | |
| I am aware of what makes my learning more effective (e.g, a place to study, time to study, etc.) | | | | |

| | | | | |
|---|---|---|---|---|
| **INFORMATION SEEKING SKILLS** | | | | |
| I am able to find a specific book or journal in the library using the on-line catalogue (Talisprism) | | | | |
| I am able to use a variety of different sources to find information (e.g. journals. books, electronic resources) | | | | |
| I am able to access and search electronic resources (on-line databases, electronic journals CD- ROMs) | | | | |
| I can use search gateways on the Internet to find information | | | | |
| I can evaluate the information I find | | | | |
| **READING AND NOTE MAKING** | | | | |
| I can decide which parts of a book I need to read | | | | |
| I have a system for recording where I find information (e.g., book, author, date) | | | | |
| I can select and use different reading strategies (e.g., skim, scan, in-depth) | | | | |
| I can make effective notes when reading | | | | |
| I can make effective notes when listening (e.g.,during lectures) | | | | |
| I have a system for recording and storing my notes | | | | |

| SKILLS AREA | I CAN DO THIS WELL | OK, BUT I NEED MORE PRACTICE | I CAN'T DO THIS | PRIORITY DEVELOPMENT OF THIS SKILL 1 = Very Important, 2 = Quite Important, 3 = Not Important |
|---|---|---|---|---|
| **WRITING SKILLS** | | | | |
| I can analyse assignment (essay, report, etc.) questions to determine what is expected | | | | |
| I understand the difference between an essay and a report | | | | |
| I can produce a written plan to answer an assignment question | | | | |
| I can punctuate, use grammar and spelling correctly | | | | |
| I am confident I can express my ideas clearly in written form | | | | |
| I am able to adapt my writing styles to suit the appropriate media/ audience | | | | |
| I understand the need to reference my work to avoid plagiarism | | | | |

| SPOKEN COMMUNICATION | | | | |
| --- | --- | --- | --- | --- |
| I am able to express my views verbally | | | | |
| I am confident speaking in front of a group of people | | | | |
| I can prepare, plan and deliver a presentation | | | | |
| I can use visual aids to support a presentation | | | | |
| I work well as a member of a group or team | | | | |
| I can listen to and appreciate the views of others | | | | |

| INFORMATION TECHNOLOGY | | | | |
|---|---|---|---|---|
| I can use a word processing software package to produce my assignments | | | | |
| I can use a variety of different computer software (e.g., Word, PowerPoint, Excel, Access) | | | | |

| WORKING WITH NUMBERS | | | | |
|---|---|---|---|---|
| I am competent in making simple calculations | | | | |
| I can present numerical information accurately | | | | |
| I can competently use a variety of numerical techniques (e.g., percentages, fractions, decimals) | | | | |
| I can interpret and present information in graphs and illustrations | | | | |

| REVISION AND EXAM TECHNIQUES | | | | |
|---|---|---|---|---|
| I can plan my revision time | | | | |
| I can set myself goals | | | | |
| I can use various revision techniques (e.g., practicing questions, mind mapping, etc.) | | | | |
| I can select and use techniques to help me retain and recall information | | | | |
| I use strategies to help me in the exam room (e.g., planning time, and coping with anxiety) | | | | |

| STRESS MANAGEMENT | | | | |
|---|---|---|---|---|
| I know what causes stress | | | | |
| I am aware of my symptoms of stress | | | | |
| I can use strategies to help me cope with my stress | | | | |

| PERSONAL DEVELOPMENT PLANNING | | | | |
|---|---|---|---|---|
| I am able to identify my personal goals | | | | |
| I am a good judge of what my strengths and areas for development are | | | | |
| I am able to identify opportunities for learning outside my course, e.g., clubs, societies, employment | | | | |
| I can plan for my personal development | | | | |

| SKILLS AREA | I CAN DO THIS WELL | OK, BUT I NEED MORE PRACTICE | I CAN'T DO THIS | PRIORITY DEVELOPMENT OF THIS SKILL 1 = very important, 2 = quite important, 3 = not important |
|---|---|---|---|---|
| **ORGANISATION OF LEARNING** | | | | |
| **I have strategies to help me to plan and manage my time** | | | | |
| **I can effectively prioritise my tasks and activities** | | | | |
| **I can work to deadlines** | | | | |
| **I am aware of what makes my learning more effective (e.g, place to study, time to study, etc.)** | | | | |

| | | | | |
|---|---|---|---|---|
| **INFORMATION SEEKING SKILLS** | | | | |
| I can find a specific book or journal in the library using the on-line catalogue (Talisprism) | | | | |
| I can use a variety of different sources to find information<br><br>(e.g., journals. books, electronic resources) | | | | |
| I can access and search electronic resources (on-line databases, electronic journals CD- ROMs) | | | | |
| I can use search gateways on the Internet to find information | | | | |
| I can evaluate the information I find | | | | |
| **READING AND NOTE MAKING** | | | | |
| I can decide which parts of a book I need to read | | | | |
| I have a system for recording where I find information (e.g., book, author, date) | | | | |
| I can select and use different reading strategies (e.g., skim, scan, in-depth) | | | | |
| I can make effective notes when reading | | | | |
| I can make effective notes when listening (e.g., during lectures) | | | | |
| I have a system for recording and storing my notes | | | | |

| SKILLS AREA | I Can Do This Well | Ok, But I Need More Practice | I Can't Do This | PRIORITY DEVELOPMENT OF THIS SKILL 1 = Very Important, 2 = Quite Important, 3 = Not Important |
|---|---|---|---|---|
| **WRITING SKILLS** | | | | |
| I can analyse assignment (essay, report, etc.) questions to determine what is expected | | | | |
| I understand the difference between an essay and a report | | | | |
| I can produce a written plan to answer an assignment question | | | | |
| I can punctuate, use grammar and spelling correctly | | | | |
| I am confident I can express my ideas clearly in written form | | | | |
| I can adapt my writing style to suit the appropriate media/ audience | | | | |
| I understand the need to reference my work to avoid plagiarism | | | | |

| SPOKEN COMMUNICATION | | | | |
|---|---|---|---|---|
| I can express my views verbally | | | | |
| I am confident speaking in front of a group of people | | | | |
| I can prepare, plan and deliver a presentation | | | | |
| I can use visual aids to support a presentation | | | | |
| I work well as a member of a group or team | | | | |
| I can listen to and appreciate the views of others | | | | |

| INFORMATION TECHNOLOGY | | | | |
|---|---|---|---|---|
| I can use a word processing software package to produce my assignments | | | | |
| I can use a variety of different computer software (e.g., Word, PowerPoint, Excel, Access) | | | | |

| WORKING WITH NUMBERS | | | | |
|---|---|---|---|---|
| I am competent in making simple calculations | | | | |
| I can present numerical information accurately | | | | |
| I can competently use a variety of numerical techniques (e.g., percentages, fractions, decimals) | | | | |
| I can interpret and present information in graphs and illustrations | | | | |

| REVISION AND EXAM TECHNIQUES | | | | |
|---|---|---|---|---|
| I am able to plan my revision time | | | | |
| I can set myself goals | | | | |
| I can use various revision techniques (e.g., practising questions, mind mapping, etc.) | | | | |
| I can select and use techniques to help me retain and recall information | | | | |
| I use strategies to help me in the exam room (e.g., planning time and coping with anxiety) | | | | |

| STRESS MANAGEMENT | | | | |
|---|---|---|---|---|
| I know what causes stress | | | | |
| I am aware of my symptoms of stress | | | | |
| I can use strategies to help me cope with my stress | | | | |

| PERSONAL DEVELOPMENT PLANNING | | | | |
|---|---|---|---|---|
| I am able to identify my personal goals | | | | |
| I am a good judge of what my strengths and areas for development are | | | | |
| I am able to identify opportunities for learning outside my course, e.g. clubs, societies, employment | | | | |
| I am able to plan for my personal development | | | | |

## *DID YOU FIND YOUR REFLECTION TO FILL THE SKILLS GAP USEFUL?*

*Feedback - remember to keep auditing your skills and upskilling.*

## CHAPTER 5

# RANGE OF LEARNING ACTIVITIES THAT A LEADER CAN USE TO IMPROVE

R ANGE OF LEARNING ACTIVITIES THAT A LEADER OR MANAGER COULD USE TO IMPROVE AND DEVELOP THEIR LEADERSHIP SKILLS TO HELP THEM DEAL WITH THE FOLLOWING SITUATIONS:

The following are useful for a leader to improve, so learning them is key to good management.

Visionary leadership - Where people share the dream. The leader can increase efficiency by moving decision making responsibility to the frontline. Achieved with limited supervision. To make frontline responsibility effective, leadership must allow workers to develop decision-making skills and learn to trust them.

Dominant belief systems and the culture norm of the workplace, which Tucker describes during forming, will play a part in this process. The leader will need to build trust and rapport in and with the team.

If during the Tucker stages of storming, where testing others in the team takes place and the norming of valuing differences is absent, then the result could be a prejudicial way of the team and even the team leader and manager feeling that other people are less capable and establish a management policy which reflects that belief.

So the group's norm, as described by Tucker, is established. If Dr. Belbin's theory is that there are different psychological make-up in people who assume roles, if this is applied to a leader who wishes to control a team, then that may lead to a self – fulfilling prophecy where workers are conditioned to do nothing unless closely supervised .

This can lower morale in a team and breed an enduring culture of fear. As Tuckman's development stages show, there will be the opposite of flexibility from the trust.

Coaching – Is the process of unlocking the potential in individuals or teams to achieve concrete business results.

## FORMING

Team acquaints and establishes ground rules. Formalities are preserved and members are treated as strangers.

## STORMING

Members start to communicate their feelings but still view themselves as individuals rather than part of the team. They resist control by group leaders and show hostility.

## NORMING

People feel part of the team and realize that they can achieve work if they accept other viewpoints.

## ADJOURNING

The team works in an open and trusting atmosphere where flexbility is the key and hierarchy is of little importance.

## ADJOURNING

The team conducts an assessment of the year and implements a plan for transitioning roles and recognizing members' contributions.

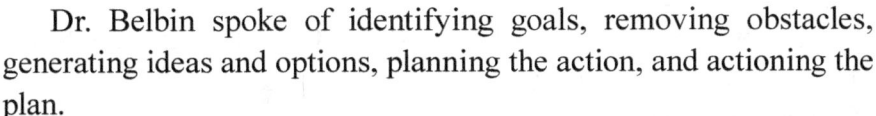

Dr. Belbin spoke of identifying goals, removing obstacles, generating ideas and options, planning the action, and actioning the plan.

The leader connects people, creates teamwork and harmony working to achieve the group's goals. Coaching can help identify the individual's talents and strengths and to value them. Coaching can get results as it focuses attention on a particular issue. It assures an understanding of the issues that cause positive shifts in thinking and behaviour.

Brain research

How it works is that brain research has shown that the brain learns best when dealing with the real world complex scenarios, which explains why coaching is so powerful.

Democratic – Inclusion and participation show that each member is valued by their leader. If the leader focuses sessions on real world issues facing the group (which are naturally complex) and thus the brain integrates new material and learning in a way that rarely happens in a classroom or lecture theatre.

By using a series of powerful, open questions to provoke a new perspective on the issues facing the client, in doing so, they coach the client to generate solutions for themselves.

Because the solution is self – generated, it is accepted and, more importantly, auctioned this is part of psychology.

The immediate application of theory to their issue assists the client learning quickly due to its relevance. This helps the team members to move forward.

Putting them into practice.

By attending seminars and industry related workshops and conferences, and a leader investing in their knowledge in these areas they can develop.

Mentoring schemes and also through action – learning it depends on the individual manager.

Some on – line courses will also be useful.

Also, undertaking the Dr. Belbin self evaluation inventory or questionnaire can enable a deeper insight into the weaknesses and strengths and the mindset of the leader and manager and also teams.

I have enclosed a copy of one of these in the book appendix.

Effective and ineffective team behaviours

These can be useful techniques and strategies for a leader to put into practice in their work environment.

1.  Solution-oriented, rather than being problem-focused. When they identify a problem with the people they manage, they can provide at least one solution. This is a more positive way of managing and leading.
2.  Seeking to have all customers and team members feel "trusted". Important, special, and pleasing. Through respectful verbal and non – verbal communication.
3.  We refrain from destructive inner – office gossip. Recognising the negative impact, this can have on a team.
4.  Having fun working together and celebrating our accomplishments.
5.  Beginning each working day with a positive greeting, recognising the first 15 minutes of the day often sets the team environment .
6.  Looking for the good and positive in people.

Observations skills to detect and analyse – Ineffective

1.  Those who do not contribute enough. "Pulling their weight".
2.  Unwilling to share.
3.  Not worthy of trust.
4.  Pursue personal goals over the team objective/ vision.
5.  Blame others and have excuses.
6.  Unduly negative.
7.  Lack of sensitivity and feelings of others.

To deal with this, the manager needs to be familiar with the psychological mindsets of people.

The Dr. Belbin module is good for this as it shows that certain team members may be best placed in certain roles.

To balance a team, we can learn how to get the best out of them. We delegate certain roles to diverse team members as managers and leaders.

We need to balance the team's weaknesses and strengths.

Seminars and training, and brainstorming with other leaders. Consulting with other managers in forums like Linkedin and other platforms like project management can also assist. No point in reinventing the wheel.

Further research and improvement, and development by setting yourself leadership plans and objectives

As time goes on, as a leader, the team will have to be monitored continuously as Tuckam has identified the stages of development. This will ensure that any changes in the team's behaviour are handled and managed as they arise.

In my opinion, it is the insight into the mind and how to get the best from people and the team's production. However, it needs careful analysis and understanding before it can be applied, as it requires a leader who will continue to develop and support individual team members. In capitalist systems, it can also be seen as a way to identify individuals' weaknesses rather than support them and coach or mentor them to exploit those in a "dog eat-dog "environment.

Therefore the theories need to be thoroughly tested and weighted against other performance indicators and practical ways of working in any organisation. It is a true mark of an organisation that protects the vulnerable members of a team and nurtures them, as diversity now means more and more companies have to ensure those with disabilities are not victimised.

Overall it is useful for any manager or leader to grasp and understand the two modules of Dr. Belbin and Tucker. I have found them extremely useful and thought-provoking research, which has stood solid over time.

The appendix questionnaire is attached below

# BELBIN SELF-PERCEPTION INVENTORY

For each section, distribute ten marks among the sentences you think most accurately describe your behaviour. These marks may be distributed among several sentences; in extreme cases, they might be spread among all the sentences, or 10 marks may be given to a single sentence. However, try and avoid either extreme. Enter the points in the INTERPLACE answer sheet provided.

*I. WHAT I BELIEVE I CAN CONTRIBUTE TO A TEAM:*

10. I think I can quickly see and take advantage of new opportunities.
11. My comments, both on general and specific points, are well received.
12. I can work well with a very wide range of people.
13. Producing ideas is one of my natural assets.
14. My ability rests in being able to draw people out whenever I detect they have something of value to contribute to group objectives.
15. I can be relied upon to finish any task I undertake.

16. My technical knowledge and experience are usually my major assets.
17. I am prepared to be blunt and outspoken in the cause of making the right things happen.
18. I can usually tell whether a plan or idea will fit a a particular situation.
19. I can offer a reasoned and unbiased case for alternative courses of action.

## II. IF I HAVE A POSSIBLE SHORTCOMING IN TEAM WORK, IT COULD BE THAT:

20. I am not at ease unless meetings are well structured and controlled and generally well conducted.
21. I am inclined to be too generous towards others who have a valid viewpoint that has not been given a proper airing.
22. I am reluctant to contribute unless the subject contains an area I know well.
23. I have a tendency to talk a lot once the group gets on to a new topic.
24. I am inclined to undervalue the importance of my own contributions.
25. My objective outlook makes it difficult for me to join in readily and enthusiastically with colleagues.
26. I am sometimes seen as forceful and authoritarian when dealing with important issues.
27. I find it difficult to lead from the front, perhaps because I am over-responsive to group atmosphere.
28. I am apt to get too caught up in ideas that occur to me and lose track of what is happening.
29. I am reluctant to express my opinions on proposals or plans that are incomplete or insufficiently detailed.

## III. WHEN INVOLVED IN A PROJECT WITH OTHER PEOPLE:

30. I have an aptitude for influencing people without pressuring them.
31. I am generally effective in preventing careless mistakes or omissions from spoiling the success of an operation.
32. I like to press for action to make sure that the meeting does not lose sight of the main objective.
33. I can be counted on to contribute something original.
34. I am always ready to back a good suggestion in the common interest.
35. One can be sure I will just be my natural self.
36. I am quick to see the possibilities in new ideas and developments.
37. I try to maintain my sense of professionalism.
38. I believe my capacity for judgement can help to bring about the right decisions.
39. I can be relied on to bring an organised approach to the demands of a job.

# BELBIN ASSOCIATES: INTERPLACE SELF-PERCEPTION INVENTORY

## IV. MY CHARACTERISTIC APPROACH TO GROUP WORK IS THAT:

40. I maintain a quiet interest in getting to know colleagues better.
41. I contribute where I know what I am talking about.
42. I am not reluctant to challenge the view of others or to hold a minority view myself.
43. I can usually find an argument to refute unsound propositions.
44. I think I have a talent for making things work once a plan has been put into operation.
45. I prefer to avoid the obvious and open up lines that have not been explored.
46. I bring a touch of perfectionism to any job I undertake.
47. I like to be the one who makes contacts outside the group or firm.
48. I enjoy the social side of working relationships.

49. While I am interested in hearing all views I have no hesitation in making up my mind once a decision has to be made.

## *V. I GAIN SATISFACTION IN A JOB BECAUSE:*

50. I enjoy analysing situations and weighing up all the possible choices.
51. I am interested in finding practical solutions to problems.
52. I like to feel I am fostering good working relationships.
53. I can have a strong influence on decisions.
54. I have a chance of meeting new people with different ideas.
55. I can get people to agree on priorities.
56. I feel I am in my element where I can give a task my full attention.
57. I can find an opportunity to stretch my imagination.
58. I feel that I am using my special qualifications and training to advantage.
59. I usually find a job gives me a chance to express myself.

## *VI. IF I'M SUDDENLY GIVEN A DIFFICULT TASK WITH LIMITED TIME and UNFAMILIAR PEOPLE:*

60. I usually succeed in spite of the circumstances.
61. I like to read up as much as I conveniently can on a subject.
62. I would feel like devising a solution of my own and then trying to sell it to the group.
63. I would be ready to work with the person who showed the most positive approach.

64. I would find ways to reduce the task size by establishing how different individuals can contribute.

65. My natural sense of urgency would help to ensure that we did not fall behind schedule.

66. I believe I would keep my cool and maintain my capacity to think straight.

67. In spite of conflicting pressures I would press ahead with whatever needed to be done.

68. I would take the lead if the group was making no progress.

69. I would open up discussions with the view to stimulating new thoughts and getting something moving.

## VII. WITH REFERENCE TO THE PROBLEMS I EXPERIENCE WHEN WORKING IN GROUPS:

70. I am apt to overreact when people hold up progress.

71. Some people criticise me for being too analytical.

72. My desire to check that we get the important details right is not always welcome.

73. I tend to show boredom unless I am actively engaged with stimulating people.

74. I find it difficult to get started unless the goals are clear.

75. I am sometimes poor at putting across complex points that occur to me.

76. I am conscious of demanding from others the things I cannot do myself.

77. I find others do not give me enough opportunity to say all I want to say.

78. I am inclined to feel I am wasting my time and would do better independently.

79. I hesitate to express my personal views in front of difficult or powerful people.

# BELBIN ASSOCIATES: INTERPLACE SELF-PERCEPTION INVENTORY, ANSWER SHEET

## BELBIN SELF-PERCEPTION INVENTORY ANSWER SHEET

| | |
|---|---|
| Last Name: | Sex: M / F |
| First Name: | |
| Organisation: | |
| Department: | Date: / / |

## DIRECTIONS:

For each section, distribute 10 points between the sentences you think most accurately describe your behaviour.

These points may be distributed between several sentences. In extreme cases, they might be spread among all the sentences, or ten points may be given to a single sentence, although try to avoid both extremes. Enter the points in the answer sheet provided.

Please allocate whole numbers only - no fractions or decimals. Please leave the box blank if you cannot assign points to a sentence.

# MARK MARK MARK MARK MARK MARK MARK

| SECTION I | | SECTION II | | SECTION III | | SECTION IV | | SECTION V | | SECTION VI | | SECTION VII | |
|---|---|---|---|---|---|---|---|---|---|---|---|---|---|
| 10 | | 20 | | 30 | | 40 | | 50 | | 60 | | 70 | |
| 11 | | 21 | | 31 | | 41 | | 51 | | 61 | | 71 | |
| 12 | | 22 | | 32 | | 42 | | 52 | | 62 | | 72 | |
| 13 | | 23 | | 33 | | 43 | | 53 | | 63 | | 73 | |
| 14 | | 24 | | 34 | | 44 | | 54 | | 64 | | 74 | |
| 15 | | 25 | | 35 | | 45 | | 55 | | 65 | | 75 | |
| 16 | | 26 | | 36 | | 46 | | 56 | | 66 | | 76 | |
| 17 | | 27 | | 37 | | 47 | | 57 | | 67 | | 77 | |
| 18 | | 28 | | 38 | | 48 | | 58 | | 68 | | 78 | |
| 19 | | 29 | | 39 | | 49 | | 59 | | 69 | | 79 | |

## TOTAL 10 10 10 10 10 10 10 70

*This SPI Answer Sheet is part of the Belbin Team Role Expert System INTERPLACE, produced by BELBIN ASSOCIATES, UK.*

# OBSERVER ASSESSMENT

| | |
|---|---|
| *Name of Assessor:* | *Name of Observed:* |
| *Organisation:* | *Organisation:* |
| *Department:* | *Department:* |

## *Date:* / / Relationship of the Assessor to the Observed: Boss/Subordinate/Colleague

| | |
|---|---|
| *Tick the words from List A that you think are descriptive of the person being observed. If you think a word is very descriptive, give a double tick (√√). Should you consider that there is a shortage of appropriate words then add some of your own.* | *Now tick any of the words in List B if you believe them to be at least partly applicable. The instructions are otherwi- se the same as for list A.* |

## DO NOT GIVE MORE THAN 33 TICKS ON LIST A (DOUBLE TICKS COUNT AS 2) or MORE TICKS ON LIST B THAN LIST A, and DO NOT GIVE MORE THAN 7 DOUBLE TICKS ALTOGETHER.

# LIST A LIST B

| | |
|---|---|
| ❏ 1 accurate | ❏ 26 knowledgeable |
| ❏ 2 adaptable | ❏ 27 logical |
| ❏ 3 analytical | ❏ 28 loyal |
| ❏ 4 broad in outlook | ❏ 29 observant |
| ❏ 5 calm and confident | ❏ 30 opportunistic |
| ❏ 6 caring | ❏ 31 original |
| ❏ 7 challenging | ❏ 32 outgoing |
| ❏ 8 clever | ❏ 33 outspoken |
| ❏ 9 competitive | ❏ 34 perfectionist |
| ❏ 10 conscientious | ❏ 35 persistent |
| ❏ 11 conscious of priorities | ❏ 36 persuasive |
| ❏ 12 consultative | ❏ 37 practical |
| ❏ 13 co-operative | ❏ 38 professionally dedicated |
| ❏ 14 creative | ❏ 39 realistic |
| ❏ 15 diplomatic | ❏ 40 self-reliant |
| ❏ 16 disciplined | ❏ 41 shrewd |
| ❏ 17 efficient | ❏ 42 single-minded |
| ❏ 18 encouraging others | ❏ 43 technically skilful |
| ❏ 19 enterprising | ❏ 44 tough |
| ❏ 20 good at follow through | ❏ 45 well organised |
| ❏ 21 hard-driving | |
| ❏ 22 imaginative | |
| ❏ 23 impartial | |
| ❏ 24 innovative | |
| ❏ 25 inquisitive | |

❏ 1 aggressive
❏ 2 critical
❏ 3 easily bored
❏ 4 empire-building
❏ 5 erratic
❏ 6 fearful of conflict
❏ 7 forgetful
❏ 8 frightened of failure
❏ 9 fussy
❏ 10 impatient
❏ 11 impulsive
❏ 12 indecisive
❏ 13 inflexible
❏ 14 insular
❏ 15 laid back
❏ 16 manipulative
❏ 17 not interested in others
❏ 18 over-sensitive
❏ 19 provocative
❏ 20 reluctant to delegate
❏ 21 resistant to change
❏ 22 sceptical
❏ 23 slow-moving
❏ 24 territorial
❏ 25 unadventurous
❏ 26 unorthodox
❏ 27 up-in-the-clouds

*This Observer Assessment Form is part of the Belbin Team Role Expert System INTERPLACE, produced by BELBIN ASSOCIATES, UK.*

# A TRAINERS GUIDE TO THE COMPLETION OF THE OBSERVER ASSESSMENT SHEETS

*Directions: Please read carefully!*

**O**bservers should be from the workplace. They may be bosses, subordinates or colleagues of the person concerned. Please obtain at least 4 persons from the workplace to complete the Observer's Assessment Forms. This will enable INTERPLACE to process a candidate's overall Team Role profile. Obtaining 6 observations per person may be beneficial, as this will allow for unacceptable observer data to be eliminated without disrupting the process. From experience, we would suggest that three of the six should be peers, if this is possible.

If the Observer Assessment Sheets are completed in an undiscriminating manner or if the Observers show excessive prejudice either in favour of or against the observed, INTERPLACE will not accept the inputs. A filter protects the system from "garbage in, garbage out" In reality, many prospective Observers need to further their observational skills to make useful assessments. As the instructions to the Observers stand, a certain percentage of assessments are likely to be lost through rejection. This can be a benefit as it means that a good measure of confidence can be placed on the assessments used.

The percentage of lost assessments can however be reduced by giving prospective Observers some preliminary training. The suggested method is to get them to work in small teams. A public personality is discussed and the group reaches some combined assessment. Care is taken to think of actual instances of behaviour to back up any conclusions reached. In this way, the skills of the prospective Observers will steadily improve.

Fewer assessments will also be rejected if Observers are given more specific guidelines. An elaborated instruction can take the following form:

> "Let's assume that we take the average of everybody in the world, then "Mr. Average" would be the same as everybody else. However, we all know that people are different, and it is this difference that we are attempting to measure. So, when you consider the statements on the Observer Sheets, you should tick only those which apply above that level. Ticking too many boxes would show that the observed is above average at most things, and should this be true, it would be very rare. Most people have some strong points and some weak points. So try to complete the form with discrimination."

Double ticks can be given when an Observer feels that the observed has an extremely strong quality.

The computer is programmed to reject those forms that do not discriminate sufficiently amongst the behaviours offered, i.e.: An excessive number of ticks on List A (over 33) or very few (less than 6)

- There must not be too many double ticks (more than 7), on either List A or B
- There must not be more double ticks than single ones
- There must not be more ticks on List B than on List A
- An excessive number of ticks on List B (over 19)

© *This Observers Trainers Guide is part of the Belbin Team Role Expert System INTERPLACE produced by BELBIN ASSOCIATES, UK.*

# CHAPTER 6

# DEVELOPING WORK PLANS

## DEVELOPING WORK PLANS THAT SUIT YOUR STYLE OF MANAGEMENT AND LEADERSHIP

**D**evelop work plans to achieve given organisational objectives—roles, workflow, aligning resources with objectives, prioritizing workloads, organizational and legal restraints.

Smart targets. Goal theory (Locke). Features of motivating goals, role of shared vision in setting objectives, balancing quality, time, quantity, and cost objectives.

Evaluate the suitability of existing quality standards for a given business activity. Product and service specifications and standards, customer orientation of quality standards.

Fit with organizational quality management systems, Key performance indicators, Total quality management, Kaizen, quality circles, quality chain, and external quality standards.

**Seven key questions**

How do we want to be seen?

What do we check against?

How are we actually seen?
How do we measure?
What is holding us back?
How can we improve?
What do we do next?

Setting smart targets

What does the smart acronym stand for?
Specific, measurable, achievable, realistic, and time-based.
It is beneficial to use planning aids for smart people to assist the organisation. These can be planners, charts, diaries, calendars, on your webpage, or intranet sites for staff to use.

Goal setting

(Locke) His theory was that there is a relationship between motivation and setting goals. His research found that there was more motivation for specific and challenging goals than in vague and easy goals.

He also found that if there was positive feedback and recognition, training and improvement this led to the empowerment of the person who set the goal/s.

The five principles he highlighted were;

1. **Clarity**
2. **Challenge**
3. **Commitment**
4. **Feedback**
5. **Task complexity**

1. Clarity

- Clear goals are measurable and unambiguous. When a goal is clear and specific, with a definite time set for completion, there is less misunderstanding about what behaviours will be rewarded. You know what's expected and can use the specific result as motivation. When a goal is vague – or expressed as a general instruction, like "Take initiative" – it has limited motivational value.

- To improve your or your team's performance, set clear goals that use specific and measurable standards. "Reduce job turnover by 15%" or "Respond to employee suggestions within 48 hours" are examples of clear goals.
- When you use the SMART acronym to help you set goals, you ensure the clarity of the goal by making it Specific, Measurable, and Time-bound.

2. Challenge

- One of the most important characteristics of goals is the level of challenge. People are often motivated by achievement, and they'll judge a goal based on the significance of the anticipated accomplishment. When you know what you do will be well received, there's a natural motivation to do a good job.
- Rewards typically increase for more difficult goals. If you believe you'll be well compensated or otherwise rewarded for achicving a challenging goal that will boost your enthusiasm and your drive to get it done.
- Setting SMART goals that are Relevant links them closely to the rewards given for achieving challenging goals. Relevant goals will further the aims of your organisation, and these are the kinds of goals that most employers will be happy to reward.
- When setting goals, make each goal a challenge. If an assignment is easy and not viewed as very important
  - and if you or your employee doesn't expect the accomplishment to be significant – then the effort may not be impressive.

3.    Commitment

Goals must be understood and agreed upon if they are to be effective. Employees are more likely to "buy into" a goal if they feel they were part of creating that goal. The notion of participative management rests on involving employees in setting goals and making decisions.

One version of SMART – when working with someone else to set their goals – has A and R stand for Agreed and Realistic instead of Attainable and Relevant. Agreed goals lead to commitment.

This doesn't mean that every goal has to be negotiated with and approved by employees. It does mean that goals should be consistent and in line with previous expectations and organisational concerns. As long as the employee believes that the goal is consistent with the goals of the company, and believes the person assigning the goal is credible, then the commitment should be there.

Interestingly, goal commitment and difficulty often work together. The harder the goal, the more commitment is required. If you have an easy goal, you don't need a lot of motivation to get it done. When you're working on a difficult assignment, you will likely encounter challenges that require a deeper source of inspiration and incentive.

As you use goal setting in your workplace, make a reasonable effort to include people in their goal setting. Encourage employees to develop their goals and keep them informed about what's happening elsewhere in the organisation. This way, they can be sure that their goals are consistent with the overall vision and purpose that the company seeks.

4.    Feedback

In addition to selecting the right type of goal, an effective goal program must also include **feedback.** Feedback provides opportunities to clarify expectations, adjust goal difficulty, and gain recognition. It's important to provide a benchmark opportunities or targets, so individuals can determine how they're doing.

These regular progress reports, which measure specific success along the way, are particularly important when it's going to take a long time to reach a goal. In these cases, break down the goals into smaller chunks, and link feedback to these intermediate milestones.

SMART goals are Measurable, ensuring that clear feedback can be provided.

With all your goal setting efforts, make sure that you build in time for providing formal feedback. Certainly, informal check- ins are important, and they provide a means of giving regular encouragement and recognition. However, taking the time to sit down and discuss goal performance is long term performance improvement. See our article on Delegation for more on this.

## 5.  Task Complexity

The last factor in goal setting theory introduces two more requirements for success. For goals or assignments that are highly complex, take special care to ensure that the work doesn't become too overwhelming.

People who work in complicated and demanding roles probably have a high level of motivation already. However, they can often push themselves too hard if measures aren't built into the goal expectations to account for the complexity of the task. It's therefore important to do the following:

- Give the person sufficient time to meet the goal or improve performance.
- Provide enough time for the person to practice or learn what is expected and required for success.

The whole point of goal setting is to facilitate success. Therefore, you want to ensure that the conditions surrounding the goals don't frustrate or inhibit people from accomplishing their objectives. This reinforces the "Attainable" part of SMART.

He also found that if a goal is too complex, it can result in;

- Disinterest
- Overwhelming
- Lack of motivation
- Resistance

Performance management

Key performance indicators (KPIs)

Performance management is the process used to manage this performance. The key question asked is, "How well is an employee applying his or her current skills, and to what extent is he or she achieving the outcomes desired?"

The answer has traditionally been found in the performance evaluation process, where managers look for hard data to determine how well employees have performed their duties.

What is often missing from this evaluation, however, is the part about making sure that the employee is doing the right thing. After all, you may have a very hard-working and dedicated team member, but what is the point if they are not working on something that advances the organisation's purpose?

This is where key performance indicators come into play and apply at the organisational and individual levels. At an organisational level, a Key Performance Indicator (KPI) is a quantifiable metric that reflects how well an organisation achieves its stated goals and objectives.

For example, if your vision includes providing superior customer service, then a KPI may target the number of customer support requests that remain unsatisfied by the end of a week. By monitoring this, you can directly measure how well your organisation is meeting its long-term goal of providing outstanding customer service.

The resulting behaviors may be counterproductive if your KPI is inappropriate or naive. For example, using the same goal of providing superior customer service, the first KPI that often comes to mind is the number of customer complaints received. Intuitively, you may feel that the fewer complaints you receive, the higher the customer service you're offering. This is not necessarily true: You may be getting fewer complaints because you have fewer customers or because customers cannot access your support services.

Taking this a step further, while organisations need to choose the correct KPIs for business performance, it is equally useful if managers and employees define KPIs for members of their teams. An ideal situation is where KPIs cascade from level to level in the organisation (in reality, this may be impractical if there are many levels in the organisation.) This helps people work in such a way that their activities are aligned with corporate strategy.

Employee Goals and KPIs

So part of performance management is setting goals with members of your team. This may be done within the formal appraisal process, but it doesn't have to be. The important factor is that the goals that are set are aligned with the department's strategy, which in turn is aligned with the overall strategy of the organisation.

This follows the common adage in management that says, "What is measured gets done." If you set a goal around a certain outcome, the chances of that outcome occurring are much higher simply because you have committed to managing and measuring the results.

When an employee's goal is defined in an organisational KPI, it ensures that what the employee is doing is well aligned with the goals of the organisation. This is the critical link between employee performance and organisational success.

Let's take an example of how an individual employee's goal is linked to organisational strategy:

- Organisational Vision – To be known for our superior customer service and satisfaction.

- Organisational Objective – To reduce the number of dissatisfied customers by 25%.
- Organisational KPI – The number of customer complaints that remain unresolved at the end of a week.
- Team Member's Goal – To increase the number of satisfactory complaint resolutions by 15% during this period.

Taken to the next level, each employee goal should have at least one associated KPI. How will you specifically measure, regularly, whether or not this person is meeting their goal?

- Team Member KPI – The weekly percentage difference in complaints handled that result in satisfied customers versus unsatisfied customers.

**Critical Success Factors** (CSFs) as KPIs are essentially a way of making CSFs measurable.

Use the following questions to help you work towards defining effective KPIs:

Understanding the context

- What is the vision for the future?
- What is the strategy? How will the strategic vision be accomplished?
- What are the organisation's objectives? What needs to be done to keep moving in the strategic direction?
- What are the Critical Success Factors? Where should the focus be to achieve the vision?

Defining KPIs

- Which metrics will indicate that you are successfully pursuing your vision and strategy?
- How many metrics should you have? (Enough, but not too many!)

- How often should you measure?
- Who is accountable for the metric?
- How complex should the metric be?
- What should you use as a benchmark?
- How do you ensure the metrics reflect strategic drivers for organisational success?
- How could the metrics be cheated, and how will you guard against this?
- What negative, perverse incentives would be set up if this metric was used, and how will you ensure these perverse incentives are not created?

KPIs and Rewards, Recognition, and Development

When satisfied that you have meaningful metrics for measuring organisational or employee performance, you now have to ensure that the supporting elements of employee performance are also aligned.

Just as what gets measured gets done, so does what gets rewarded!

When establishing your rewards and recognition practices, ensure that what you are rewarding ties directly to the KPIs you set. For example, if you are measuring people on how well they deal with customer complaints, rewarding them for lowering the number of complaints confuses the message you're trying to send.

Conversely, if your organisation wants to attract new customers, you might have a KPI that measures how many new customers are attracted each week. Depending on the situation, a well-aligned performance system may reward employees based on the number of new customers they help to attract.

The use of formal performance measures is one approach to managing performance. However, don't forget the importance of inspiration and good leadership!

Key Point

KPIs are metrics that link organisational vision with individual action. If you think of strategic practice as a pyramid, as shown in Figure 1 below, with vision at the top and actions at the bottom, in the middle, you find the KPIs derived from the strategy, objectives, and critical success factors of the organisation.

**Figure 1:**
How Individual Actions link to Organizational Vsion via KPIs

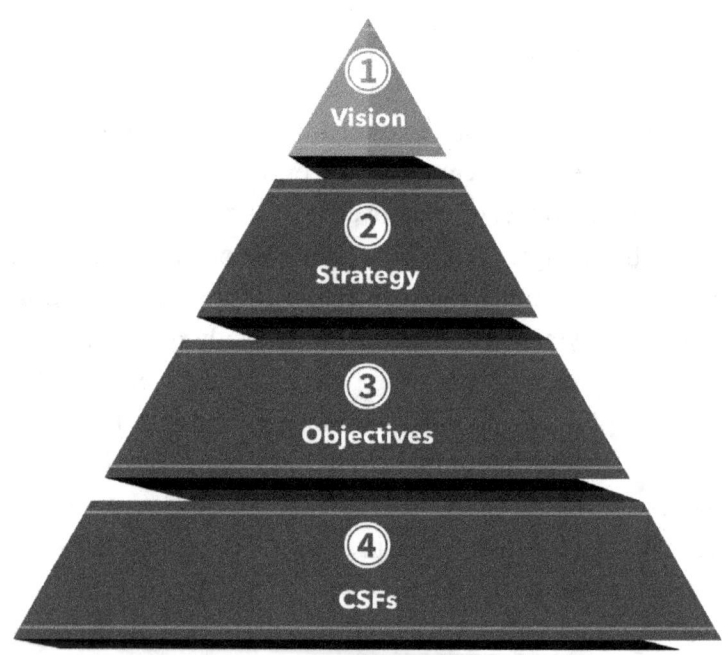

Below the KPIs are the activities and projects that are pursued by the organisation in an attempt to achieve the KPIs.

To ensure that these activities align with the organisation's strategy, you must concentrate on what the employees do.

You do this through performance management. By applying the principle of KPIs to employee goals and performance, you create a direct link between the key success factors derived from the overall strategy.

The result is that members of your team actually do what they should be doing, and that your measurements for determining how well they are doing are tied to organisational success.

## KAIZEN

It was developed in Japan following World War II. The word Kaizen means "continuous improvement." It comes from the Japanese words ("Kai ") which means change or to correct, and ("Zen,") which means good.

Kaizen is a system that involves every employee, from upper management to the cleaning staff. Everyone is encouraged to come up with small improvements and suggestions regularly.

This is not a monthly or once-a-year activity. It is continuous. Businesses in kaizen are always looking for ways to improve processes to help quality. In Japanese companies, such as Toyota and Cannon, a total of 60 to 70 suggestions per employee per year are written down, shared, and implemented.

In most cases, these are not ideas for major changes. Kazan is based on making little changes regularly. Always improving productivity, safety, and effectiveness while reducing waste.

Employee involvement

Those involved in production and operations are vital in spotting improvement opportunities for quality and identifying quality problems.

Kaizen teams or quality circles

These are defined as a group of workers who do similar work and who meet. Voluntarily, regularly. Usually, in normal working time, under the leadership of their supervisor.

To identify, analyse and solve "work-related" problems, also recommending management solutions.

Successful quality circles suggest that there are no formal rules. However following guidelines are often suggested;

1. The circle should not get too large. Otherwise, it becomes difficult for some circle team members to contribute effectively.
2. Meetings should be held away from the work area. So that team members are free from distraction.

The importance of customer-supplier relationships is "quality chains."

Total quality management focuses strongly on the importance of the relationship between customers, external and internal, and suppliers. These are known as "quality chains." They can be broken at any point by one person or one piece of equipment, not meeting the customer's requirements.

Failure to meet the requirements in any part of a quality chain has a way of multiplying. Failure in one part of the system creates problems elsewhere, leading to more failure and problems, so the situation is exacerbated.

Edward Demmin taught this theory all over Japan after the war. The Japanese workforce absorbed this culture at a time when they were in flux and primed for change.

Modern quality management systems encourage everyone in the workplace to think about quality in everything they do. Every employee is encouraged to think about final consumers and place them at the heart of the production process.

When a firm is certified to International Standard ISO 9001, the certificate indicates to potential customers that the organisation has continual improvement processes to enhance customer satisfaction. From this, consumers can reasonably infer that such businesses can deliver the promised quality product or service consistently.

Continual improvement of the quality management system involves:

Managing by systems and operating through processes

- identifying current and future customer requirements and meeting them
- Continually improving management systems: measuring, monitoring, analysing, and improving.

BSI supports applying quality management systems and standardisation throughout the supply chain. This can be achieved by designing and implementing a single quality management system that can apply to product or service standards for all activities within a business. The single management system can also incorporate other management systems standards that contribute to sustainable development and corporate social responsibility.

Management systems can be applied to quality, environment, risk, information security, and health and safety. For example, the Environmental Management System standard, ISO 14001, helps organisations to manage their environmental impact, such as the control of waste and pollution activities at every stage of production.

The management systems can be used in any combination as one system or alone. The audit system leads to certification and can be applied to a combined system or one. Each standard has a common structure: plan, do, check, and act.

There are several standards for manufacturing different glass bottles, such as carbonated soft drinks, and compliance with them enables production consistency in the glass industry. This also helps British glass manufacturers to meet the safety standards that retailers are looking for.

UK legislation used to require manufacturers to comply with European Union Directives and standards is a good way of doing this. A good example is the Directive for electrical equipment related to safety standards for household equipment such as televisions, DVD players, and vacuum cleaners.

Again, and happily for even the most inquisitive DIY person, modern standards require that consumers cannot easily reach the parts of domestic products with high voltages so that electrocution risks are minimised.

BSI's stakeholder approach means that consumers' views have high priority. When, for example, consumers complained that the outside of some toasters became dangerously hot, new standards of heat installation were introduced.

Establishing clear standards creates order in an increasingly complex world. Standards meet changing market needs and are customer driven.

Businesses benefit from standards because they establish ground rules that help to guarantee quality. Achieving certification to a standard might add reassurance for its customers and enable a business to boost its sales performance.

Consumers benefit because their safety and their satisfaction are both greatly enhanced. Governments benefit because such measures contribute to greater productivity and economic growth, and safer work, leisure and home environments.

The new ISO 26000 Standard, published in November 2010, guides the underlying principles of social responsibility, the core subjects and issues of social responsibility, and how to integrate socially responsible behaviour into existing organisational strategies, systems, practices, and processes. By looking at an organisation's behaviour, the ISO 26000 Standard evaluates to what extent it transparently and ethically:

- Contributes to sustainable development, including the health and welfare of society.
- Takes into account the needs and expectations of stakeholders.
- Is compliant with applicable laws and consistent with international norms.
- Integrates and implements these behaviours throughout the organisation.

**Achieving organisational objectives**

Work plans provide a framework for planning and serve as a guide during a specified period for carrying out work. An organisation's commitment to planning can be measured by how it completes work plans to reach each strategic goal and determines various methods to verify and evaluate the actual implementation of the work. Organisations should have annual work plans for each unit that corresponds to their fiscal year. The work plan includes a schedule of events and responsibilities that details the action to be taken to accomplish the goals and strategies laid out in the strategic plan. The core of an organisation's annual work plan consists of objectives developed to be consistent with the goals and strategies of the strategic plan. These objectives are specific, concrete, measurable statements of what will be done to achieve a goal and state what will be accomplished by when and by whom, generally within a one-year timeframe.

What Is a Work Plan?

In constructing an overall work plan, it is important to consider linking the strategic plan to daily operations. This requires a realistic view of the scope of work to be undertaken by linking planned actions to available resources. A work plan should be developed for every major unit of the organisation and each employee. The employee work plans should depict how the organisation's overall work plan will be implemented.

The Alliance for Nonprofit Management (www.allianceonline. org) suggests including the following characteristics for an effective work plan:

- An appropriate level of detail enough to guide the work, but not So much that it becomes overwhelming or confusing or Unnecessarily constrains creativity.

- A format that allows for periodic reports on progress toward the Spccific goals and objectives.

- A structure that coincides with the strategic plan goal Statements for the strategic plan and the work plan is one and The same, but objective statements are different.

Evaluation is an important part of any work planning. If you possibly can, take the time to develop an evaluation/assessment strategy that ties key measures of success to the major goals and objectives included in your work plan—this will make it easier to track progress and celebrate successes, both during the project and after your project is complete.

Evaluation Planning Tips:

- Create your evaluation plan before starting the implementation
- Decide what to measure to track your progress for each objective – the ideal is to measure the top level outcome you are

trying to achieve (greenhouse gas emissions prevented, energy conserved). In addition, it is useful to measure the behaviour changes needed to achieve these outcomes. The closer your indicator is to your desired outcome, the better information you will have about how well you achieve your primary goals.

- Determine if you have baseline data. If you know where your metrics are before the project starts, it becomes much easier to measure change and impact.
- Set an evaluation timeline and include a corresponding data collection schedule – e.g., "I want to make this much progress towards this objective by this date."
- Look for trends in the data and be willing to course correct if the data is pointing you down a different path.

Below is a sample evaluation checklist populated with potential climate action campaign goals and objectives. It is helpful to create a separate checklist for each overall goal and its supporting objectives for any particular project.

| Sample Evaluation Checklist | | | |
|---|---|---|---|
| Goal: *Engage community members to join together to impact climate change.* | | | |
| | **Measured by?** | **Goal?** | **By when?** |
| **Objective1:** *Reduce City's carbon footprint.* | *Greenhouse gas emissions* | *Reduce by X%* | *One year from campaign completion* |
| **Objective 2:** *Build an engaged, motivated community of citizens for climate action.* | *Participation in Greenpeace or other climate action campaigns* | *5,000 citizens sign up for the campaign* | *One year from campaign launch* |
| *Objective 3: Motivate citizens to take climate-saving actions.* | *Sales of energy-efficient products (CFLs, appliances, etc.)* | *X% sales increase at major local retailers* | *Within 18 months of campaign launch* |

Developing Work Plan Elements of a Work Plan The text of the work plan comprises several sections: introduction, background, goals, objectives, outputs, resources, constraints, strategy, and actions. An effective work plan may look like this:

## 1 Diagram below

**The work plan is divided up into different colours showing the Smart targets and the process and tasks required to disseminate activities to deliver the project's work plan.**

**The arrows and directions of them show the connection.**

**This particular work plan illustrates the environmental sustainability of the European food and drink chain.**

**Part of the seventh framework program of the European commission.**

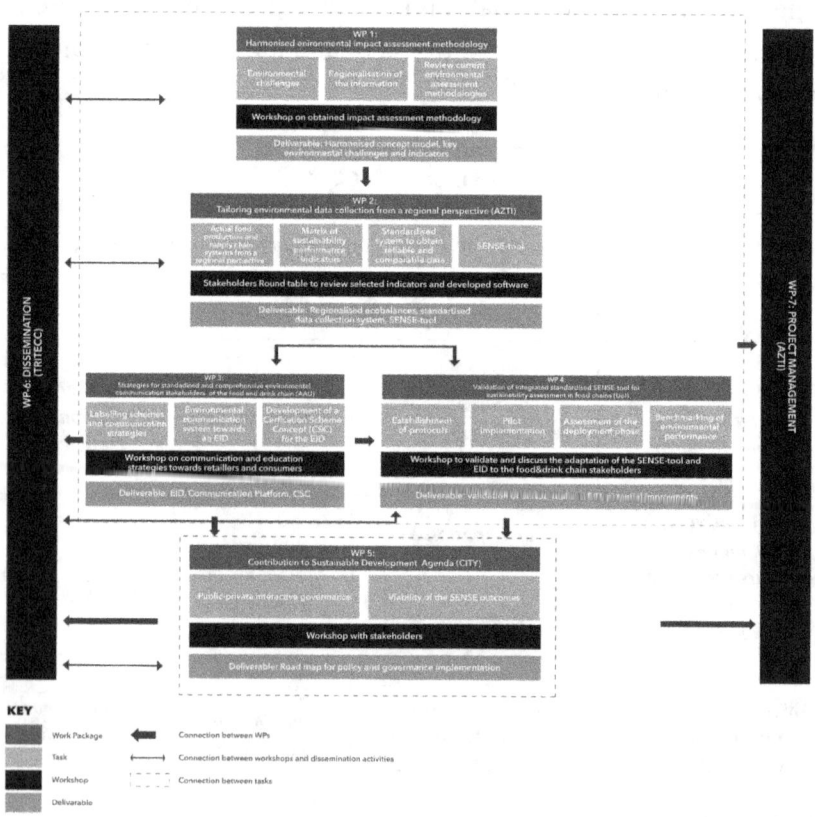

- ○ Abstract or executive summary
- ○ Introduction and background (identifies the problems)
- ○ Goals and objectives (defines the solutions; refines the goals)
- ○ Resources and constraints. These can include financial as well as legal restraints.
- ○ This could be health and safety laws. (Indicates what is available to reach
- ○ The objectives)
- ○ Strategy and actions (indicates how the resources will be converted to objectives, then goals)
- ○ Appendices (budget, schedule, and other useful information)

## Abstract or Executive Summary

Write this part last, and make sure it is a summary, not an introduction. Ideally, this should be one or two paragraphs long, covering half a page.

## Introduction and Background

Do not copy or repeat the background information of the strategic plan—that was useful for justifying the overall program but not for the specific time segment of the work plan. In the "Background" section of the work plan, include only information or references that refer specifically to those outputs and objectives you wish to achieve during the period covered by the work plan.

The background should contain the following:

- ○ Information gleaned from the previous quarterly report, especially the recommendations
- ○ Any relevant changes in conditions in the environment that may or already have affected operations
- ○ Any relevant effects or results of activities that may call for changes in operations or the design of activities· Any other

references that will justify the selection of objectives and outputs for the planned period.

Goals and Objectives

The work plan should have a logical progression from the introduction and background to the goals and objectives. Where the background explains the selection of the problems to be solved, the goals define the solutions to those problems. The objectives, then, are more precise, finite, and verifiable derivations of the goals.

Keys to Developing Objectives and Timelines

- While identifying objectives, keep them realistic by asking if this can truly be accomplished.
- Integrate the current year's objectives as performance criteria in each "implementer's" job description and performance review.
- Remember that objectives and timelines are only guidelines, not rules set in stone. They can be deviated from, but deviations should be understood and explained. Resources and Constraints

The "Resources" section should indicate what may or will contribute to reaching the identified and selected objectives. Include resources that are not necessarily liquid cash at this time, such as staff and other personnel (e.g., volunteers); partners (organisations and individuals); consultants; land; capital; supplies; equipment; additional inventory that can be used, sold or traded; and anything else that can be mobilised and utilized in reaching the identified objectives.

The "Constraints" section should identify any restrictions or hindrances that must be overcome to reach the objectives. Please include a short description of how to overcome them.

Strategy and Actions

The "Strategy" section should indicate how to convert resources and overcome constraints, using those identified inputs (resources) to reach the objectives or attain the outputs specified. Actions primarily belong to strategy because they are the activities that convert inputs into outputs. Where the goals and objectives are among the project's outputs, the resources are among the inputs.

Appendices

Appendices supplement the text, providing details that support the argument. Budgets and schedules are among such details.

The work plan for each major unit and employee might specify the following:

- o  The goal(s) that are to be accomplished
- o  How does each goal contribute to the organisation's overall strategic goals
- o  What specific results (or objectives) must be accomplished that, in total, reach the goal of the organisation
- o  How will those results be achieved
- o  When the results will be achieved (or timelines for each objective)

Work Plan Accountability

It is important to develop a process for tracking the progress of the work plan. Ideally, this occurs quarterly. During the tracking process, identify if an action has been completed, is in progress, is delayed, or if there is a barrier. Early identification of problems and early intervention ensures that the work plan keeps moving forward. It is also important to highlight successes and celebrate them.

## Quality involves everyone

Quality is not just the concern of the production or operations department.

Marketing Finance
Human resources

It involves all the above as well as production or operations.

**Quality -The measure of excellence or being free from defects, deficiencies, and significant variations".**

*What do you check against?*

Focus on your policies, processes, and procedures.
Ensure you communicate openly and honestly.
Develop a set of quality standards with which to measure your performance.

## Total quality management

Principles of TQM

1. Be Customer focused: Whatever you do for quality improvement, remember that ONLY customers determine the level of quality.

    Whatever you do to foster quality improvement, training employees, integrating quality into processes management, ONLY customers determine whether your efforts were worthwhile.

2. Ensure Total Employee Involvement: You must remove fear from the workplace, then empower employees... you provide the proper environment.

3. Process Cantered: Fundamental part of TQM is to focus on process thinking.

4. Integrated system: All employees must know the business mission and vision. An integrated business system may be modelled ISO 9000

5. Strategic and systematic approach: Strategic plan must integrate quality as a core component.

6. Continual Improvement: Using analytical, quality tools, and creative thinking to become more efficient and effective.

7. Fact-Based Decision Making: Decision-making must be ONLY on data, not personal or situational thinking.

8. Communication: Communication strategy, method, and timeliness must be well defined.

At its core, Total Quality Management (TQM) is a management approach to long–term success through customer satisfaction.

In a TQM effort, all members of an organisation participate in improving processes, products, services and the culture in which they work.

The methods for implementing this approach come from the teachings of such quality leaders as Philip B. Crosby, W. Edwards Deming, Armand V. Feigenbaum, Kaoru Ishikawa and Joseph M. Juran.

A core concept in implementing TQM is Deming's 14 points, a set of management practices to help companies increase their quality and productivity:

1. Create constancy of purpose for improving products and services.
2. Adopt the new philosophy.
3. Cease dependence on inspection to achieve quality.
4. End the practice of awarding business on price alone; instead, minimise total cost by working with a single supplier.
5. Improve constantly and forever every process for planning, production, and service.
6. Institute training on the job.
7. Adopt and institute leadership.
8. Drive out fear.
9. Break down barriers between staff areas.
10. Eliminate slogans, exhortations, and targets for the workforce.
11. Eliminate numerical quotas for the workforce and numerical goals for management.
12. Remove barriers that rob people of pride in workmanship, and eliminate the annual rating or merit system.

13. Institute a vigorous program of education and self-improvement for everyone.
14. Put everybody in the company to work accomplishing the transformation.

From my research for this work unit, "Total Quality Management" has lost favour in the United States in recent years: "Quality management" is commonly substituted. "Total Quality Management" is still used extensively in Europe.

# CHAPTER 7

# COOPERATIVE AND COLLABORATIVE MODELS OF MANAGEMENT AND LEADERSHIP

C ooperative management is effective and purposeful relationship between management .

Co-management tries to achieve more effective and equitable systems of resource management. Representatives of all groups, the stakeholder's cooperative management model is that which shares knowledge, power, and responsibility in cooperative or co-management.

The profit the owners make is not transferred or invested into the workers, but rather any surplus profits are distributed to the owners, and the workers' wages are regulated.

In the Cooperative model or a community trust model, the profits are shared with all the staff, and they each receive a dividend.

The objective of cooperative management is to achieve common goals.

To utilise resources.
To fulfill social obligations.
To maintain economic growth.
To improve the knowledge of workers.
To meet the challenge of the business model change.

The Co-operative business model is used widely in various countries and by various industries like healthcare in Spain and Italy. Or financial cooperatives like the London community credit union I established in 2000 in London, UK.

In the UK, the largest cooperative is the Coop group, which has retail shops, funeral care, and insurance services.

A cooperative is an autonomous association of persons united voluntarily to meet their common economic, social, and cultural needs and aspirations through a jointly-owned and democratically controlled enterprise.

Membership in a cooperative society should be voluntary and open.

With equitable participation and control among all concerned in the enterprise.

COOPERATIVE PRINCIPLES AND VALUES
SUCCESS OF THE COOPERATIVE

**Four Pillars of Cooperative Governance**

Democratic member control is one of the main aspects of the business model. It distinguishes cooperative business and can be applied uniformly to any cooperative.

When it comes to leadership and managers in a cooperative, another distinctive feature is that members select among themselves their own leader, who they can also remove democratically.

The one member, one vote is the form of democracy adopted by cooperatives.

This eliminates the possibility of a few people who, by their shareholdings, control the company's assets.

A cooperative treats members as human beings and not as subscribers of capital.

Economic participation

The annual surplus is the excess income over expenditure for a financial year. Often cooperatives decide to distribute such surplus; the distribution must be based on members dealing with the cooperative society and is not distributed based on the number of shares held as in a capitalist business.

The profit is viewed as belonging to those whom it has been derived, and that is to whom it should be returned.

The ICA commission states that share capital shall receive a strictly limited interest rate, if any. There is no co-operative principle that obliges interest to be paid on share capital; the rate should be limited and fixed on the ground that the supplier of capital is not equitably entitled to share in savings, surplus, or profit.

The main objective of the Cooperative is to ensure the evolution, promotion, and defence of health cooperatives.

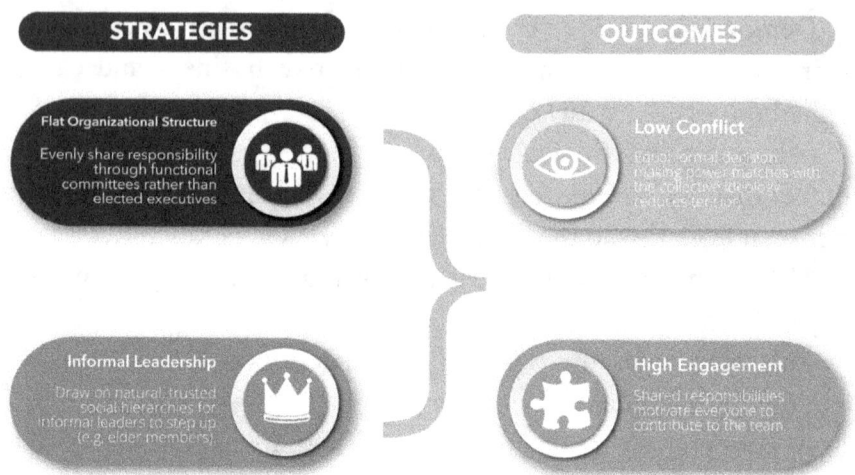

Autonomy and independence:

Cooperatives are Autonomous, self-help organisations controlled by their members. If they enter into agreements with other organisations, including governments, or raise capital from external sources, they do so on terms that ensure democratic control by their members and maintain their cooperative autonomy.

Cooperate among cooperatives

The principle of co-operation among cooperatives is essential for the survival and maintenance of the growth of the co-operative movement. ICA Commission, 1966, stated, "All cooperative organisations, to best serve the interest of their members and their communities, shall actively cooperate in every practical way with other co-operatives at local, national, and international levels."

Cooperative education

The ICA rules provide that "all co-operative societies shall make provisions for the education of their members, officers and employees and the general public, in the principles and techniques of co-operation both economic and democratic."

Concern for community

Cooperatives work for the sustainable development of their communities through policies approved by their members.

Organisation Structure examples.

Medical cooperative Fundacion Espriu in Spain during covid treated more than 20,000 patents.

The Espriu foundation was created on the 17th of February 1989 and brings together Spanish institutions that practice the cooperative healthcare model created by Dr. Josep Espriu, a health service delivery system based on an organisational vision of health. Open to solidarity and shared management.

Thus constituting a forum for knowledge about the problems and solutions necessary to advance in the improvement of health [protection systems.

Its activities are aimed at representing health cooperatives, research and dissemination of cooperative health management, and the training of professionals.

It is a member of the International Cooperatives alliance.

Management structures

Management of a cooperative, when a few co-op members have executive power, the rest of the group will also have less ownership. It may result in other co-op members being less motivated to work on common goals and to engage in group activities.

Introducing formal hierarchies into cooperatives can be problematic.

It can create a mismatch between the "unequal" control that the structure attracts. And the "equal" ownership that co-ops rely on.

It can create confusion among members, which raises questions about status, task division, and how they resolve differences.

Co-ops with established executive roles have high levels of conflict, compared to those with flatter structures in which responsibilities are more evenly distributed across members.

Two models of governance are Hierarchical and Flat.

The Hierarchical is with an executive team composed of a chairperson, vice chair, secretary, treasurer, and recruiter organiser. These roles are all elected by the membership.

With a flat structure of co-op management, a committee structure co-op members are delegated committee roles, like finance or marketing, on a rotating basis and coordinate with other committees.

Flat governance in a cooperative often leads to more engaged members and less conflict and the members feel they have more of a stake in the cooperative business.

There is no one leader, and they all work together as members.

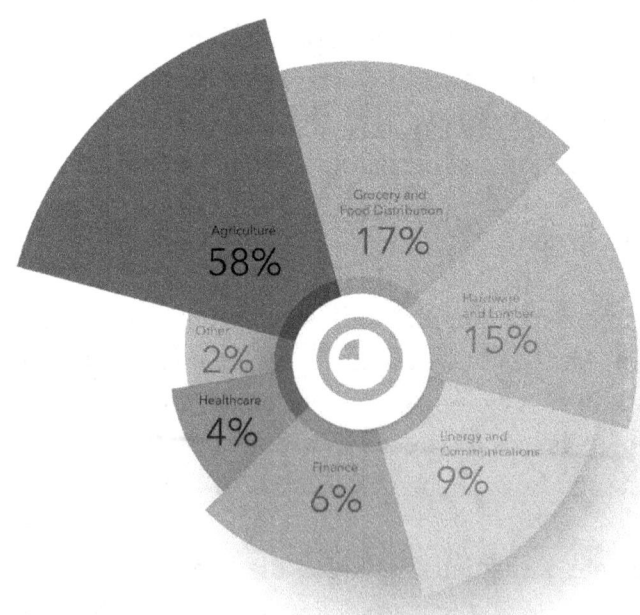

Co-operative Group Limited, trading as Co-op, is the largest British consumer co-operative with a group of retail businesses, including food retail, wholesale, e-pharmacy, insurance and legal services, and funeral care.

They are one of the world's largest consumer co-operatives, owned by more than 5 million members.

They are the UK's fifth biggest food retailer, with more than 2,500 local, convenience, and medium-sized stores. Its other wholly-owned businesses are the UK's number one funeral services provider.

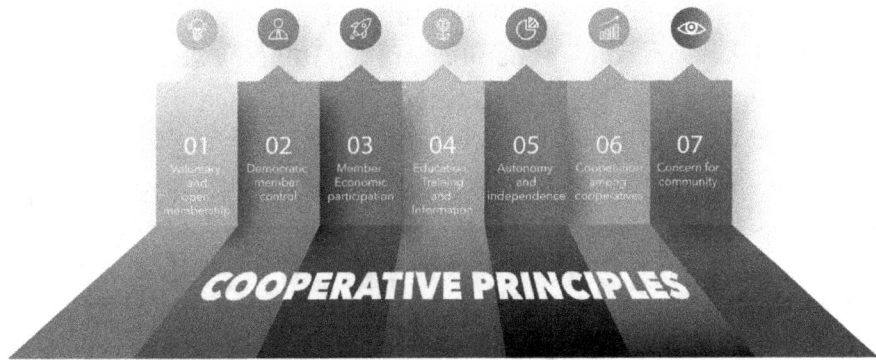

The Co-operative Group has its origins in Rochdale, Lancashire. The Rochdale Pioneers Society was famously established in 1844 based on ethical trading and the belief that business profits should be shared amongst members according to their purchases.

The Co-operative Wholesale Society (CWS) was formed in 1863 by independent co-op societies to provide Co-op produced products to sell in hundreds of Co-op stores that had opened based on the Rochdale model of ownership and control.

By 1900 there were over 1,400 independent co- operative businesses in the UK, all members of a wider Co- operative Movement.

During the 1900s, many of these independent societies began to merge. One of the most significant in recent times was in 2000 when The Co-operative Group was formed following the merger of the Co-operative Wholesale Society and Co-operative Retail Services. This was followed in 2007 by the merger of United Co-operatives with The Co-operative Group.

Member-owned model

Membership lies at the heart of their business. Members and businesses own them for their benefit in accordance with Co-op Values and Principles.

Along with all co-operative societies, The Co-operative Group is democratically controlled by its members. However, they differ from most other UK consumer co-operatives in that they have independent society members and individual members.

Anyone can become a member of the Group by subscribing for a £1 share. The Co-operative Group is jointly owned by millions of individual members and Independent Co-operative societies.

They listen to members' opinions and integrate these into their business activities and our social and campaigning agenda.

The equitable nature of The Co-operative Group is exemplified through the opportunity for every member to get involved in running the business. In addition to having the right to vote on a one-member, one vote basis, each member has the right to stand for election on either the Group Board or Council.

I am a member of the national member council of the Co-operative group in the United Kingdom.

Social goals

The Co-operative Movement was founded to serve a social purpose as well as a commercial one. They are guided by the long-established co-operative values of self-help, self-responsibility, democracy, equality, equity, and solidarity, alongside their commitment to ecological sustainability and social responsibility.

Cooperatives are active worldwide; they are thriving in Europe, America and Africa and range from agriculture, banking and retails. According to the International Labour Organisation. 100 million people are employed worldwide, and the livelihoods of nearly half of the world's population depend on them.